Yes, You Can Be Cabin Crew!

The perfect springboard to a new career as a cabin crew member

Introduction

Hello and welcome to *Yes, You Can be Cabin Crew!* I'd like to congratulate you on taking a positive step forward to realize your dream of becoming a cabin crew member. My name is Shon and I am the founder member of Ready to Fly Ltd. Your personal guidebook should provide you with the inside info' you'll need to prepare yourself for the airline interview.

During my long career as a senior cabin crew member with British Airways, I was also involved in recruitment and training all new recruits to the airline. The skills, knowledge and extensive experience I have gained during my employment with British Airways has been encapsulated into this unique guidebook, to help you to prepare for your own success.

Although I stopped flying 5 years ago to spend more time with my young family in Devon, my enthusiasm and passion for this exciting industry has never waned and since then I have been writing and presenting cabin crew preparation programmes to hundreds of applicants to the airline world, every year.

The overall theme of this guidebook is about preparing for success and if you take the concepts outlined and translate them into your world you should certainly achieve the outcome you desire and will be living your dream sooner than you think.

Good luck in pursing your chosen career!

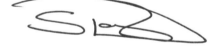

Table of Contents

A career as cabin crew

The Job

Becoming a cabin crewmember is an exciting prospect. It's a career that has the power to transport you from the dull routine and predictable work patterns of a normal everyday job, into a world of excitement, challenge and endless opportunity. No wonder it's sought after by thousands of people, every year.

Every day is different; every flight, unique and one of the most exciting aspects of the job is the regular contact and interaction you have with such a huge range of different people. You have lots of opportunities to get close to some of your favourite celebrities too. You'll look out of the window to a view that changes by the minute! Wonderful!

When work is over you may be in a different county or different country where your time is your own, able to choose what you want to do: from visiting the local attractions, meandering the colourful shopping streets, or simply lazing by the pool. What a great way to spend your working life!

Put simply, working as a cabin crew member is a fantastic experience and although you will always be very busy, I promise you will never be bored!

On the down side, (after all – nothing's that good!) working as a cabin crewmember is a very demanding role. People's expectations are higher than ever before, which means they are now much more willing to complain when things don't go right. You'll be expected to placate and win them over – even though you may feel like spitting in their dinner at times!! You'll be constantly pushing heavy trolleys against the force of gravity; sometimes working very long hours; you'll be eating when you should be sleeping; you'll also be permanently living out of a suitcase, and you'll be away from home most weekends. If you are the sort of person who hates leaving loved ones behind, then you'll need to seriously consider whether the lifestyle will be right for you, as the lifestyle of a cabin crew member can put a big strain on even the most stable of relationships.

Through my flying career with British Airways, I have been privileged to enjoy one of the most rewarding and glamorous jobs that I could ever have hoped for and have been totally spoiled by the unique lifestyle that this career brings. I hope that this book is able to bring you the same.

Qualities of a Cabin Crew Member

You as a Person

To be successful at an airline interview will require your ability to show the recruitment team that you are that special person with many or all of the qualities detailed on the next page. A person who will fit in well with their existing teams on board and the person that their customer wants to do business with.

You will need to show the interviewer that you are able to communicate well with people of all ages, from all parts of the world and the interview process has been designed to carefully test your skills in these areas. You will be expected to demonstrate a genuinely friendly and caring personality; a mature and organized approach to work; an ability to remain calm under pressure, and the ability to work well in a team environment, contributing towards the overall performance and success of each flight.

Generally, airlines look for candidates who are:

- Friendly and caring personality.
- Competent in handling difficult situations.
- Confident communicator and great listener.
- Supportive of colleagues and a team player.
- Able to remain calm and efficient under pressure.
- Willing to treat everyone as an individual.
- Satisfy current BA/CAA health requirements.
- Takes pride in personal grooming with no visible tattoos or piercings and willing to conform to uniform standards.
- Able to swim well with confidence.
- Be prepared to work unsociable hours any day of the year, at any time, including weekends and public holidays.
- Able to work to tight time constraints.
- Can meet the mandatory requirements for Cabin Crew

The Rewards of the Job

In return for your dedication and commitment to the role of cabin crew you can expect many rewarding benefits which include some or all of the following:

- A totally flexible work pattern that breaks away from the routines and confines of a 9-5 job

- A generous salary, usually higher than the average wage

- The chance to meet and work with new friends regularly

- The provision of first class hotel accommodation when you are away from home

- Opportunities for concessionary travel – for you and members of your family – around 90% discount

- A job with a real difference

- An exciting career that offers something different every time you go to work

- Opportunities to explore many countries, enjoying cultural, geographical and social differences that each one has to offer

To prepare yourself well for a cabin crew interview it is important that you undertake some sort of analysis of yourself. Read through the important qualities of a cabin crew member, below, and then complete the short exercise over leaf:

QUALITIES OF A CABIN CREW MEMBER

Intelligent	Enthusiastic	Confident	Cheerful	Motivated
Caring	Patient	Helpful	Articulate	Look Good
Dependable	Attentive	Friendly	Supportive	Honest
A great sense of humour		Robust & Resilient		

EXERCISE:

Write down at least 3 qualities that you feel are your strengths:

1.

2.

3.

Write down 3 qualities that you feel you need to work on:

1.

2.

3.

"It's a fabulous job,

everything you said it was and more.

I'm so happy!! "

Andrew Isles
Cabin Crew
British Airways

"I love my job as a nurse but in my heart I have always wanted to be cabin crew. The Ready to Fly Course left me feeling in no doubt that this was the right choice"

Marylou Paras
Course Delegate
May 2005

The Right Airline

Decide which airline you'd be happiest working for.

When I was applying to become an air stewardess, many years ago, there were only a handful of airlines to choose from. The 21st century however, brings you a much larger choice of airlines: From scheduled operators to holiday airlines all providing domestic, European or international services. Each airline has its own product; from a no-frills experience, through to a high quality service; As a result, you, the applicant can choose from a variety of working lifestyles.

Some points worth considering when deciding which airline would be right for you are the following:

- Are you prepared to be away from home for several days at a time or would you be happier just operating local holiday flights – there and back in a day?

- Would you prefer to work for an airline that operates a Charter service or are you more interested in the Scheduled travel market?

- How important is the airline's image to you? Do you prefer Virgin's fresh, modern, innovative brand or easyJet's more informal, low cost image?

- Do you want to be part of a smaller airline or a global carrier?

Once you know the answer to these questions you can begin to whittle down the airlines that meet your own requirements, and then set about applying to them. Details of all the major European airlines are listed on pages 143 to 156.

EXERCISE:

Ask yourself the following 2 questions and don't just think the answers in your head, write down your answers: Your answers will help you when it comes to answering the same interview questions

Why do you want to become a cabin crewmember?

What do you want from the job? (travel; fun; long term career; sophisticated image; chance to meet exciting/famous people etc?

'I had no idea what to expect at an airline interview. 'Yes You Can Be Cabin Crew' takes away the mystery of the cabin crew recruitment and provides you with the knowledge that builds self-confidence to be fully prepared for the entire process"

Pedro Miguel
Cabin Crew
British Airways

The Airline Selection & Interview Process

The cabin crew selection and interview process has been carefully designed to select the best possible candidates for the job, the airline and their customers.   To do this efficiently and effectively, most cabin crew interviews comprise 3 or 4 stages.

To be successful at an airline interview you will need to pass all 4 stages and to do that, you will need to convince the recruitment team that:

1. You have the necessary skills and qualities that they are looking for and have demonstrated these well during the selection process;

2. You have an outstanding ability to work well in a team; and

3. You can deliver the excellent standard of customer service that their customers expect.

The stages will usually include some or all of the following:

1st Stage: Application form

2nd Stage: Documentation check; Height & Weight check and general ability tests involving general knowledge, numerical skills and personality tests.

3rd Stage: Self – introduction and Team Assessments - Group exercises

4th Stage: Personal interview, Medical examination, Language assessment (if applicable) Reference clearance and Criminal Record checks.

1st Stage

If you pass the 1st stage (the application form) you will be invited to attend an interview to participate in stages 2,3 and 4.   You should expect the interview day to last between 3 and 6 hours (depending on the airline and your success through each stage).

2nd, 3rd and 4th stage

All applicants attending a cabin crew interview will be asked to participate in one or more of the next 3 stages (2, 3, and 4) completing one stage at a time.   Each stage should last no longer than 40 minutes.   If you are successful in stage 2 for instance, then you will be asked to participate in stage 3 and so on, until the final stage, the personal interview.

The 1st Stage Completing an airline Application form

"The Ready to Fly Cabin Crew Preparation Course showed me how to use the right words to match my current skills and experience effectively. I've just landed my dream job with British Airways"

Hanna Norris
Cabin Crew
British Airways

Airline Application Form - 1st Stage

You'd probably be quite astounded to learn that more than 90% of applications get rejected because they are simply irrelevant, badly presented or do not demonstrate a sound understanding of what excellent customer service really is.

You need to ensure your application form will get the attention of the recruitment team and better still, guarantee you'll be invited for an interview.

1. RELEVANT EXPERIENCE:

A good starting point is to firstly ensure that you list the relevant skills and experience you have gained in your current or previous employment and match these as much as you can to the role of cabin crew. This may seem as though I am stating the obvious, but you'd be amazed at how many people fail this simple task.

Consider the following two examples which describe the duties and responsibilities of the same job very differently:

Example 1

Job Title: Hotel Receptionist.

Duties include: Front house representative;   Handling reservations; answering the telephone; handling cash; taking orders for restaurant bookings; arranging taxis for guests;

This example certainly shows exactly what the duties involve, but fails to match the skills and experience gained to those of a cabin crew member. Compare this to the second example.

Example 2

Job Title: Hotel Receptionist.

Duties include: Working in a small team to deliver an excellent service to customers; Welcoming guests; meeting and exceeding customers expectations; dealing with any guest queries; providing fast and efficient check-out service to guests; answering incoming and external calls; liaising with housekeeping and other departments to provide excellent service to guests and projecting a professional image of the hotel at all times.

2. CUSTOMER SERVICE SKILLS

This is another important section on your application form and therefore requires the finest attention to detail. On the Virgin Atlantic and British Airways cabin crew application forms there will be a question relating to customer service asking you to give an example of when you have given or received either excellent or poor customer service. The question asked will be something like this:

"Please briefly relate a recent experience where you were especially pleased with the service/assistance you were able to give someone."

When writing down your example it is important to be as concise yet detailed as possible. The following guidelines should help you:

State the fact (briefly) – i.e. what actually happened.

Describe your actions – what you did?

Describe the outcome

Explain how your actions affected your customer/affected the outcome

The 'Tingle' Factor

The recruitment team is looking for you to illustrate very effectively a clear picture that demonstrates your understanding of the effects of excellent customer service. An example that will show your feelings and concerns and demonstrate to the reader, the interaction was a positive experience for the customer/receiver. You've got to write it in a way that will produce the 'tingle' factor! You want to make the reader think: "ah, that was a really lovely thing to do" or "Oh, how thoughtful!" etc.

Example 3

Service Example: "Recently a lady called our office to say that she was very annoyed as she hadn't received the phone she had ordered from us. She had been put through to different departments and nobody was giving her answers. I checked our system to see what had happened to the order and then I called the phone delivery dept and got them to check the details and chase the order up. She received her order shortly afterwards and thanked me for my help. I felt very pleased that I had been able to assist this lady."

This example certainly doesn't give the reader that 'tingle' factor! Whilst it's evident the applicant acted swiftly in sorting the problem out, the example fails to illustrate the required empathy and emotions involved that demonstrate what they were feeling at the time of the interaction. Furthermore, it highlights the fact they were re-active rather than pro-active.

Now look at the example below and notice the phrases in italics which indicate empathy, care and excellent customer service.

Example 4

Service Example: "Recently at work I answered a telephone call from a German doctor who wanted to discuss matters relating to her imminent relocation to the UK. While talking to her *I could sense that she was feeling very apprehensive* about the relocation as it was her first time to England and she did not know anyone. *I could imagine how stressful it might be for her* and *I tried to think of what I could do to help reduce her worries.* When she told me her flight time was 7.15pm, I realized that she would arrive after work hours, so I could go and meet her at the airport and drive her to her new home. I told her my plans and she was ecstatic to know that she wasn't going to be on her own. The day the doctor was arriving, I went directly to the airport after work to meet her. When she came through the arrivals hall at the airport and saw me, the look of relief on her face was very rewarding. I felt really pleased that with just a little extra effort, I had made such a difference to help make someone feel safe and welcomed."

This example shows that the person giving the service had a clear understanding of how the situation was affecting the customer; it shows that the person delivering the service cared and illustrates that they were prepared to put themselves out and that nothing was too much trouble.

Other questions asked on cabin crew application forms

1. How does the experience you've gained in your working career match the skills required to be a cabin crew member?

    An appropriate and relevant response might be something along the lines of:

    I am used to working in small/large teams of people /Working flexible shifts/delivering a high standard of service to customers/dealing with angry customers/ looking after small children/work as part of a team/ recognize the importance of image etc.

2. Which skills and qualities can you bring to the role?

    An appropriate or typical response might be worded as follows:

    I have the ability to work well with others; ability to communicate with people at all levels; ability to recognize the importance of customer retention; ability to manage tricky situations and achieve a successful outcome; Have extensive training in First aid; Have worked in hospitals; hotel; etc then list all your personal qualities e.g. friendly, enthusiastic, motivated, supportive, cheerful, hard working etc

PRESENTATION WRITING SKILLS

Many airlines now require you to complete an on-line application form. (Refer to Airline Contact Details).

On-line applications make form filling so much easier for you and for the airline! However, it is important that your application is presentable and professional so do remember to double check for typing errors and make sure that your grammar is correct etc. Do not write in the same style that you would a phone text.

Should you be required to complete a manual paper application form that requires long hand, you will need to ensure that your handwriting is neat and presentable with no crossings out and no mistakes. If you are concerned about the neatness of your own handwriting, then consider asking a friend to fill out the form for you because if your handwriting and/or grammar are poor, you could be reducing your chances of being invited to attend an interview.

EXERCISE:

Complete the exercise on the following page. Think about a time when you've provided excellent customer service or felt you've really made a difference to someone – either at work or outside of work. What was situation, how the other person was feeling and what you did that made that person feel special. Write your example under Additional Information.

Application for Employment

Name of Employer	Job title and Responsibilities	Reason for leaving
	Relate your job responsibilities to those of a cabin crew member: e.g. *Responsibilities include: working as part of a team to deliver excellent customer service. Duties include, welcoming customers, handling cash transactions, dealing with enquiries, etc*	

ADDITIONAL INFORMATION

Please briefly relate a recent experience where you were especially pleased with the service/assistance you were able to give someone. (Please continue on a separate sheet if necessary)

Preparing for your cabin crew interview

"The 2 day training ensured that I was so well prepared for the big day. I felt quite guilty when I saw the other applicants looking and feeling so nervous!"

Sean Holtom
Cabin Crew
Virgin Atlantic

"I didn't need to waste time researching information that wasn't necessary — in addition to this, the tips and advice provided in respect of what to wear etc were great and I put the black interview suit aside — which definitely paid off!"

Martina Hozakova
Cabin Crew
British Airways

Preparing for the Interview

If you have completed an application form and you've been invited along for an assessment day or an interview – congratulations. The quality airlines have a very strict application screening process so you can give yourself a pat on the back for winning yourself an interview.

Don't be fooled into thinking that just because your application form has been successful, you can go along to the airline interview and bluff your way through it. Cabin Crew Recruitment Teams are highly experienced and well trained to extract specific information from you to determine whether you are the right person to join their team of cabin crew.

It's vital that you take steps to prepare yourself well. This section outlines some effective ways of ensuring that you've prepared yourself well and that it won't be your name they call out to tell you you've been unsuccessful!

Whilst no company will expect you to have an in-depth knowledge of their company, unless you've worked for them before of course, they will expect you to have done some research and be able to show your interest and enthusiasm for their product, achievements and future goals.

EXERCISE:

Choose an airline that you are interested in applying to and complete the Airline Research exercise on the next page. By answering the questions asked you will have all the necessary information that an airline will expect you to know about them and their industry. You may need to use the Internet, a Travel Agency or even the library to get the correct information.

To further increase your industry and airline knowledge, listen to the news; visit their website; encourage your friends/family to bring back airline literature from their travels. Ask your friends or work colleagues to describe their holiday flight experiences with the various airlines so you can compare how different airlines operate.

Airline Research

1. What's the main role of a cabin crewmember?

2. How long have they (the airline) been in operation

3. How many employees do they (the airline) have;

4. Where do they fly to?

5. Who are their share holders?

6. What are their future plans for expansion?

7. Who are their main competitors?

8. What is their Mission Statement? E.g.

   - Virgin Atlantic: "to grow a profitable airline, where people love to fly and people love to work"

   - British Airways: To be the world's undisputed leader in world travel

9. What is their product? Are they in the scheduled service market or the holiday market? Is their emphasis on turnover and quick profit? E.g. No frills airline? Or is quality branding, frequency and range of destinations of more importance? Do the offer just one class of cabin. E.g. Economy? Or have they got a choice of cabins? First Class/Upper Class/ Clubworld; Premium Economy etc

10. What recent projects have they recently undertaken or are recently undertaking that you are aware of? E.g. have they been on the national news or national newspapers?

11. What challenges does their airline face in the future? (Rising fuel prices; increased competition; remaining innovative to meet current market trends etc).

Having researched some background on this airline, what has impressed you about the company? Or what are you unimpressed with?

"I have to admit – when I think of First Impressions, especially for an interview – I'm thinking, 'nice hairdo, smart outfit and carefully applied make-up', so I hadn't really thought about my body language too much – after all that comes naturally, doesn't it?

So this part of the course was really useful. It made me much more aware of how I look to others but more importantly, what my body language was saying about me and how I was feeling today"

Mary Avis
Cabin Crew
British Airways

First Impressions

Airlines have a very clear idea about the image they want to portray to their customers and they will be looking to see that you, the applicant, can re-enforce the professional and corporate image that their customers can identify with. So before you even think about tests, and of passing or failing them, you need to be focusing on the image you want to present to the airline.

Recent surveys have discovered that many interviewers have usually decided whether you are right for the job within the first few seconds of meeting you. That's quite a thought isn't it? 90% of us actually form a first impression within the first 10–40 seconds of meeting someone and the other 10% of us make up our minds about someone else in less than 10 seconds! So it doesn't take a genius to work out the amount of time you have to create the right first impression.

The most influential form of communication you have is your body language as it represents more than half the message you are sending out. So, make your body language work for you!

EYE CONTACT

It has been said that more jobs are lost from lack of eye contact than from lack of experience or qualifications. Therefore, eye contact is not an option - it's essential! Ensure that you give everyone you meet, sincere, direct eye contact. If you are a naturally shy person, you may find eye contact extremely difficult. However, the airlines are looking for confident people so you need to look confident.

SMILE

Think about how you feel when someone smiles at you. It usually makes you feel happy, even though it may only last for a moment. Also, how do you feel when you smile? A smile is seen as welcoming. It shows you are friendly, approachable and interested. It will also encourage other applicants to want to talk to you which will also make you look good.

MOVE WITH ENERGY AND ENTHUSIASM

To show your enthusiasm and natural energy, you need to walk tall, hold your head up, shoulders back and tummy tucked in! Look confident and believe in yourself.

LISTEN WELL

To be interesting, you need to show that you are interested. So show people that you are listening to them by giving them your full attention. Make the other person feel you value what they have to say.

ENTHUSIASM

The overriding quality that recruitment teams look for in potential applicants is a natural enthusiasm. Enthusiasm is like a disease; it is catching, positive and negative, rubbing off on all those you come into contact with.

The most effective way you can show your enthusiasm at your interview is to look and sound interested throughout the interview day – even when you are feeling under pressure, show your enthusiasm by smiling as much as possible, sounding as cheerful as you look!

DON'T BE LATE!

It may sound startlingly obvious to you but it is essential that you arrive at your interview early – Not only will this enforce your enthusiasm but will also demonstrate your reliability.

The airline business is geared completely around TIME, providing a reliable and punctual service to their passengers. Believe me when I say they've heard every 'late' excuse in the book. One thing is for sure, they will not be impressed with excuses like: "the train was late"; "I couldn't find anywhere to park"; "I got lost"; "there was an accident on the motorway". They will expect you to have prepared yourself for these normal eventualities and planned your journey time sensibly around this.

I always added an hour to my journeys to and from the airports, just to give myself that extra cushioning of time in case I got held up in traffic etc. So try to allow extra time to get to your interview, to cover for the unexpected. Check out your route, and the location of the interview.

If you are going to be late, for whatever reason make sure that you advise them immediately. If you have a genuine reason why you are delayed for your interview the recruitment team will demonstrate the appropriate understanding towards the situation and make allowances.

"My family and friends suggested that I should choose something formal for my interview so when Shon suggested a more colourful suit, I was intrigued. I took Shon's advice and went along in a pale pink tailored suit...... and hey, everyone apart from me was dressed in black or navy so I definitely stood out....and I got the job as well!"

Charlotte Bhasi
Cabin Crew
British Airways

What to Wear for the Interview

What to Wear For Your Cabin Crew Interview

Whatever your friends', family's or next door neighbours' views are on the nature of the job, the airline industry is still regarded by many as one of glamour and excitement.   Most people do get excited when they go on a flight simply because it's not something that they do every day.   It becomes a special event.

As the face of the airline, cabin crew are required to help support that image of glamour.   Therefore at your cabin crew interview, how you dress is going to be extremely important.

It never failed to surprise me during my interviewing days, how often the interview room resembled a funeral gathering rather than a collection of individuals looking to join the exciting and glamorous world of flying. Almost every applicant dresses in black! You want to look good and you want to be able to stand out from the crowd so be a little bolder in your choice of outfit and do follow the guidelines on the next pages.

FEMALES:

A Smart and Professional Suit: Skirt/dress or trouser suits are acceptable. Choose something to wear that is well tailored, well fitting and something that you feel good wearing. Although the interview commands a formal suit, the nature of the industry allows you to be a little braver with colours so don't be afraid to introduce colour to your outfit.   Most applicants wear grey, navy or black to their interview and, quite honestly, it does become rather boring to the eye. So by wearing another colour like red, cream, lilac or blue, then you would instantly stand out from the crowd. Avoid wearing fabrics that crease easily otherwise you may end up looking like a crumpled mess.

Hands/Nails: Your hands will be continually on show as a crew member so the interviewers may ask to see them.   Ensure you have well manicured nails; if possible, use a nail varnish to provide that elegant finishing touch.

Tights/Stockings: Attention to detail is critical so when aiming to create a sophisticated image, you must wear tights or stockings. This rule applies even in the summer months.

Shoes: A formal court shoe is preferred. However, if you are wearing trousers then boots are acceptable. Make sure that your shoes or boots are well polished and smart looking – no scuffed edges, or tatty heels showing.

Hairstyles: Your hair is your framework, rather like that of a picture, so style it in a way that builds your confidence. If you have long hair, don't feel you have to wear it up for the interview. If the interviewers want to see how you look with your hair tied up, then they will just ask you to sweep it up during the personal interview. The most important tip is to feel good with how you look.

Your hair should look well styled and freshly washed. Do make sure that coloured or bleached hair is natural looking with no root growth and if you do decide to wear your hair up make sure there are no strands or straggly bits sticking out ANYWHERE.

Make-up: The interviewers generally like to see female applicants wearing makeup which lends a more sophisticated and glamorous image. If you don't like wearing make-up or have very little experience applying it, practise using the various cosmetics available or have a free make-up session at your nearest boutique to learn how to use make-up that will compliment your skin tone and colouring. It could be fun!

MALES

A Smart and Professional Suit: Choose something that is good quality, well tailored, and fits you well so that you'll feel good wearing it. Select a shirt that looks crisp, clean and smart. Try to avoid fabrics that crease easily otherwise you may end up looking very crumpled.

Tie: Wear a tie that denotes the formal occasion yet is able to portray your personality.

Hair: Your hair should be well styled and freshly washed. If you are tying your hair back, it is essential that it is groomed in a sophisticated way. This means no loose bits hanging down. Do make sure that coloured or bleached hair is natural looking with no root growth. Avoid outrageous colours or styles.

Facial hair: Male cabin crew are not normally permitted to wear a beard so I would recommend that you attend your interview cleanly shaven.

Hands & Nails: Hands and nails should be clean and nails, short – not bitten. Since the nature of the work involves having your hands on display at all times, the recruitment team may ask to see them.

Shoes: Ensure your shoes are clean, tidy and well polished.

MALE AND FEMALE

Jewellery: If you like to wear a lot of jewellery, you'll need to limit it to just one or two pieces for your interview. No eyebrow, lip, tongue or facial piercing is allowed – If you do have these remove these before your interview.

Tattoos: Visible tattoos are not acceptable. If you do have them, hide them if possible.

"Even though I'm a fairly confident person I've always hated having to stand up and speak in front of others. This part of the course was brilliant in helping me to prepare a little self introduction about myself that would interest others and show my outgoing and enthusiastic personality"

Jamie Latter
Cabin Crew
Virgin Atlantic

Prepare a Mini Presentation

If you have done your airline research, you should have all the information about the airline you are being interviewed for, you can now take some time to think about the interview day itself.

At the beginning of your interview day, the airline will introduce their company to you and outline the role and contract of a cabin crew member. Before or after this presentation each applicant is expected to introduce themselves to the recruitment team and the other applicants. This provides the recruitment team with a first glimpse of your personality and your confident nature.

Example of mini self- presentation:

"Hi everyone. My name is Mary and it's really nice to meet you all. I'm (x) years of age. I live in (where you live) and I currently work as a travel consultant for a firm in (wherever). It's a job I really enjoy because I have a lot of face to face contact with customers which is important to me. One of the most rewarding aspects of my job is helping people choose the right holiday and then hearing about their great experience when they get back. To know they've really enjoyed themselves really is very satisfying and makes me feel that I've done my job well.

I love living life in the fast lane and will always rise to a challenge! My scariest experience recently was doing a Bungi jump for Charity. I closed my eyes all the way down but I was thrilled to raise £2,000 for cancer research."

This example shows a highly positive and enthusiastic attitude right from the start. She personalizes her greeting by addressing everyone. She focuses on the very enjoyable parts of her work and then creates instant interest with her listeners. This style of approach will definitely catch the attention of everyone who is listening – including the recruitment team!

The information you should consider for your self-introduction is as follows:

- Your name and where you live/ where you are from.
- Current occupation and what your own role/responsibilities are
- Any hobbies or achievements that may interest others or a claim to fame

TIP: Make your short presentation enjoyable for others to listen to, using humour or any other rapport building technique to assist you, ensure that your tone of voice portrays your natural cheerful enthusiasm.

2nd stage

(The interview)

General knowledge

And

Maths tests

"Knowing exactly what to expect at each stage of the interview really helped me to feel much more confident about the whole interview day. I not only knew the order of how things would run, I practically knew what colour lipstick the interviewer would be wearing!"

Steph Lowe
Cabin Crew
Virgin Atlantic

Your Interview: The Order of Events

BRITISH AIRWAYS INTERVIEW   -   Duration: 3 ½ hours

Candidates attending a British Airways assessment day will take part in the entire assessment process – there are no candidate eliminations.

1. Document and passport check followed by candidate height measurement; seatbelt fastening and unfastening check

2. BA Presentation by recruitment team and self introduction followed by questions and answers from candidates to the recruitment team

3. Team assessment (20 minutes)

4. Personal interview (30 – 40 minutes)

With BA you may have your personal interview before your Team assessment.

VIRGIN ATLANTIC INTERVIEW –Duration 2-6 hours

Candidates attending a Virgin Atlantic assessment day should understand that they must pass each assessment before proceeding to the next one or they will be eliminated and sent home.

1. Applicant document check; height and weight check

2. Short presentation of Virgin by recruitment team: working life; duties; shifts; pay

3. Self introduction & assessment on why you want to be a cabin crew member

4. Applicants to read news sheet

5. Team assessment

6. Memory Test. You will be asked to read a passage from a sheet of paper and then recite back what you have remembered – followed by your Personal Interview – 2-1

BMI INTERVIEW –Duration 2-6 hours

Candidates attending a BMI assessment day should understand that they must pass each assessment before proceeding to the next one or they will be eliminated and sent home.

1. Document check; height and weight check; and Welcome
2. Short presentation of BMI: working life; duties; shifts; pay
3. Self introduction & assessment on why you want to be a cabin crew member
4. Maths test and General Knowledge test
5. Customer service role-play, demonstrating your ability to handle very tricky customer situations
6. Team assessment - usually involves building something out of newspaper and cellotape
7. Personal Interview – 2-1

BRITANNIA / MONARCH / MY TRAVEL / EXCEL / FIRST CHOICE / AIR ATLANTA INTERVIEW –Duration 2-6 hours

Candidates attending a Britannia (Thomson Fly) Monarch, My Travel, Excel Airways, First Choice or Air Atlanta assessment day should understand that they must pass each assessment before proceeding to the next one or they will be eliminated and sent home.

1. Document check; height and weight check; and Welcome
2. Short presentation of airline: working life; duties; shifts; pay
3. Self introduction & assessment on why you want to be a cabin crew member
4. Maths test and General Knowledge test
5. Team assessment
6. Customer service role play (demonstrating your ability to handle difficult situations well)
7. Personal Interview – 2-1

Documentation and Tests - 2nd Stage

What happens when you arrive at your interview?

There will be a member of staff to greet you and sign you in at the reception. You will be asked to produce your passport and National Insurance Card as well as all qualifications/certificates that you have said you possess. It is important that you take along all the documents that they have asked for because if they are not able to check your paperwork, they could terminate your interview at this very early point.

Height and Weight Criteria

A member of the recruitment team will then take you into a separate room where you will be measured against their criteria. This part of the process can be strict so ensure that the information you have given on your application form is correct. If your height and weight do not meet their requirements, it is likely that they will terminate your interview at this stage.

Company Presentation and Self introduction

Once you have passed the document checks, all applicants will be assembled together in one room where you will be asked to introduce yourself to the rest of the group. (See Self Introductions). You will then normally be given a brief presentation about the airline.

General Knowledge and Maths test

After all the personal introductions are over, most Charter and Budget airlines give you a general knowledge paper and maths test to complete in a certain amount of time. The tests usually last no longer than 30 – 40 minutes. The pressure that these 'test' situations often generate can be mind numbing, so it's important to maintain a positive attitude and approach the task in a confident manner. Answer the questions you find easy first and leave all the tricky ones until the end. That way, you can be confident that you have answered as many questions as possible.

Before you attend your interview it's a good idea to ensure you are familiar with capital cities of the world, current affairs, e.g. which party is in government at the time of your interview, who the cabinet ministers are etc. It's also useful to know the currencies of some of the Mediterranean countries along with other countries such as Australia, Europe and South America.

Tests

When it comes to sitting tests there aren't many people that don't tremble silently with fear that they simply aren't going to know the answers to all the questions. So this part of the cabin crew process can be really nerve racking.

British Airways and Virgin Atlantic do not give the general knowledge or maths tests. Airlines that use this type of recruitment assessment are usually the charter and budget airlines such as Monarch, Thompson fly, My Travel, First Choice and Excel Airways.

The General Knowledge tests have been designed to identify your understanding of what's going on in our current world. Airlines like to recruit people who are able to converse easily with a variety of different people from different social backgrounds and different levels of intellect etc. It's useful then to have a good general knowledge in geography, local and world politics and certainly the travel and tourism industry.

The Maths test is designed to determine your ability in simple calculations and currency conversions. The exercises contained within this section should help you to practice your numeric skills in preparation for this part of the assessment process.

EXERCISE:

Practice the general knowledge test and maths test on the next page that simulates the typical airline test. No more than 20 minutes is allowed for each test.

General Knowledge Test

Please answer as many questions as you can in 20 minutes, writing your answers underneath the appropriate questions. Answers can be found at the back of book.

1. When it is 1700 hours British Summertime in the UK, what will the time in New York be?

2. What do the letters BBC stand for?

3. Virgin Atlantic has its own airline code prefix. What is it?

4. What is the currency unit of Thailand?

5. How many European countries are members of the EU?

6. Which is further south, Malta or Tunisia?

7. Which airline operates flights on behalf of Thomson Holidays?

8. Name at least three other transport types that the airline industry competes with.

9. Which airline is Britain's national flag carrier?

10. Which month of the year is the State Opening of Parliament?

11. How many duty free cigarettes can you bring back from a non-EU country?

12. A Cabin crewmember is employed by an airline to provide an in-flight service to passengers. What is the other important role a cabin crewmember plays?

13. Which is the highest mountain in the world?

14. What is the Capital of New Zealand?

15. How many States make up the USA?

16. Name one country where females must wear an Abaya when in public?

17. In relation to time, what do the letters UCT stand for?

18. What is celebrated on the 4th July in the USA?

19. When serving a blind passenger a meal, how would you explain to them where each food item was on the plate?

20. What is the name of Africa's highest mountain?

21. Which is the busiest airport in the world, in relation to international passengers?

22. How many terminals does London Heathrow have?

23. What are the two terminals at Gatwick called?

24. The Heathrow Express is: (tick the correct answer)

    (a) Airport coffee

    (b) Airport newspaper

    (c) Airport train service

25. How many runways does Heathrow have? (tick correct answer)

    (a) 2

    (b) 3

    (c) 4

26. What is the BAA? (tick correct answer)

    (a) British Aviation Authority

    (b) British Airports Authority

    (c) An organization devoted to the welfare of sheep

27. What do the letters ATC stand for? (tick correct answer)

    (a) Air Training Corps

    (b) Air Traffic Control

    (c) Air Terrorists Campaign

28. What is the currency used in Portugal?

29. How many engines does a Boeing 747 have?

30. Since the events of 9/11 (Twin Towers) airlines must now adopt a strict security policy when recruiting staff. Can you describe 2 procedures that airlines must carry out when recruiting cabin crew?

Maths Test

If you are anything like me, as soon as anyone starts talking multiplication and long division numbers, there is an immediate danger that you'll freeze like a rabbit in headlights! However, you don't need to worry too much, the maths questions that you will be asked aren't that difficult. As long as you can add up and take away and convert different currencies using a calculator, I'm sure you'll be fine.

A word of caution though, you should aim to achieve a 50% or higher pass rate or else they may fail you.

THE USE OF CALCULATORS

The recruitment team won't normally allow you to use a calculator to work out your basic maths questions. However you are usually allowed to use a calculator to work out your currency conversions.

EXERCISE

Without using a calculator, have a go at some of the problems below: Then complete the currency conversions on the next page.

Addition	Subtraction	Multiplication	Division
1) 22+8+6=	1) 21-13=	1) 12x6=	1) 66÷6 =
2) 553+12+91=	2) 32-8=	2) 64x8=	2) 80÷4=
3) 354+253+935=	3) 762-432=	3) 23x7=	3) 868÷8=
4) 11+3+36=	4) 734-321=	4) 45x3=	4) 4567÷7=
5)1234+12+615=	5) 913-746=	5) 435x8=	5) 546÷8=
6)43+654+99999=	6) 64532-7544=	6) 2341x8=	6) 1432÷11=

Answers can be found at the back of the book.

Currency Conversions

Below are a few currency conversions that are in typical interview format. The good news is that you will be allowed to use a calculator to work the answers out. Please try to complete each one. There is a currency conversion table at the foot of the page. Answers are at the back of the book.

1. A passenger buys 200 cigarettes for £15.00 and a bottle of perfume for £24.00. She offers you 100 Australian Dollars. How much English change would you give her?

2. A passenger buys 4 alcoholic drinks at £2.00 each and 3 soft drinks at 75p each. He offers you 20 Euros. How much English change do you give him?

3. A passenger buys: 1 Aftershave at £17.00, 1 Perfume at £32.00 and 3 Cartons of cigarettes at £15.00 each. He offers you 200 US Dollars. How much is this worth in pounds and how many pounds does he need to pay?

4. A passenger buys 3 drinks at £2.00 each, 6 soft drinks at 75p each, 1 litre of Gin at £8.00, 1 litre vodka at £8.00 and 1 carton of cigarettes at £15.00. He has £22.50 in Sterling and wants to pay the rest with Malaysian Ringgits. How many Ringgits will he need?

5. A passenger buys some duty free: 1 Parker pen at £28.00, 2 litres of Scotch at £11.00 each, 3 perfumes totalling £75.00 and 1 soft toy at £6.00. She offers 700 Hong Kong Dollars and £62 sterling. How much extra will she need to pay by credit card to make up the difference?

6. A passenger purchases 2 litres of malt whisky @ £15.00 each, 3 perfumes totalling £75.00, 1 Swatch watch @ £6.00 and 1 Hermes scarf @ £90.00. He offers 75 Euros, 33 pounds Sterling, $25 U.S. dollars and wants to pay the remainder with his credit card. How much will this be in pounds sterling?

Currency Exchange Rate Table

Currency	Exchange rate
Euro	1.50 = £1.00
Malaysian Ringgit	7.00 = £1.00
US Dollar	1.80 = £1.00
Australian Dollar	2.50 = £1.00
Hong Kong Dollar	14.00 = £1.00

The 3rd Stage
Team Assessments
And team tasks

"Having been a policeman for 25 years where good teamwork is the order of the day I just couldn't understand where I had gone wrong at this stage of my Virgin interview. The Ready to Fly course not only showed me exactly what the recruitment team were looking for during this stage of the assessment, they provided plenty of practice with quality feedback which was invaluable"

Andrew Isles
Cabin Crew
British Airways

The Team Assessment - 3rd Stage

If you pass the 2nd stage – well done, you will now be invited to take part in a team assessment.

Recruitment teams like to see a lot of enthusiasm and a positive confident approach to any task. The quicker you can demonstrate this, the more interest you'll attract!

Team assessments are a popular and valuable part of selection not only in Airlines but in countless other companies too. All applicants who pass the general knowledge and maths test will usually be invited to participate in the group team task.

Team assessments are designed to draw out various people skills such as how you interact with others, what part you play in a team and how well you listen and respect other's views.

The usual format is that a small number of people (usually 5 or 6) are given a task that involves making decisions in a matter of minutes.

The selection team will observe the discussion and not take part. The topic or task may be unrelated to the job and is often quite artificial.

The whole situation is of course very false but if you are going to stand a chance of being selected then you have to take part!

It's useful to note here that the recruitment team aren't necessarily expecting the team to arrive at the perfect solution – although they would like to see evidence that your team can be an effective team. They are more interested at this point in how much you participate, how well you listen and what part you play in the group. If you are too bossy, too opinionated, fail to take notice or recognize contributions from your team mates it could go against you.

I must emphasise here that every group is different, so the observers do not expect the same reactions from each one.

The following page outlines a typical assessment that you may be given at your cabin crew interview and may be totally unrelated to the industry.

Team Assessment Example

You are cabin crew on board a Virgin Atlantic Flight from LAX to LHR.

All your passengers have been boarded onto the aircraft but you have just been informed that your flight has been delayed by 3 hours due to a technical fault with the aircraft.

Nothing works on the aircraft; there is no in flight entertainment and no power.   All passengers must remain in their seats.

Your task is to come up with some creative ways of amusing your passengers.   You can either select from the picture cards provided or come up with some ideas of your own.   You have 20 minutes to complete the task.

Forget company rules or policies – allow yourselves to be as creative and as fun as possible to ensure passengers are entertained during this 3 hour delay.

At the end of 20 minutes you must present back to the interviewer what you have chosen and why.

Picture cards include the following items:

Polo Mints	Megaphone	Playing cards	String	Golf club
Blanket	Cutlery set	Football	Hairbrush	Plastic cups
Headphones	Newspaper	Globe of world	Kettle	Dictionary
Socks	Crayons	Mirror	Oranges	Plain paper

Behaviours required for Team Assessment

As the team assessment takes place, the interviewers will be assessing you on the following behaviours

POSITIVE BEHAVIOUR	NEGATIVE BEHAVIOUR
Smiled consistently and used positive eye contact, showing continual interest	Didn't smile much – not much eye contact. Seemed detached from the team.
Able to create an immediate rapport with group	Remained quiet and reserved. Didn't join in very much
Showed an ability to help problem solve in an enthusiastic way	Wasn't able to offer any problem solving. Unable to demonstrate enthusiasm.
Showed a positive attitude towards the task offering useful contributions	Did not contribute ideas to group
Makes effort to mix with all of group	Found it difficult to mix with group
Uses appropriate sense of humour	Sense of humour was not appropriate to group or task
Listens, understands and accepts others opinions: nodding in agreement – checking own understanding	Was too bossy or too controlling. Didn't listen very well to what others had to say
Built on what others said: E.g. "X's idea would be great because……"	Disagreed/ argued with other team members. Made no positive comments when other team members offered ideas.
Gave positive comments e.g. "that's a great idea!" or "I like that idea!"	
Is able to manage pressure of task well – showing flexibility and a willingness to change	Was unable to manage the pressure of the task well and remained fixed on one idea
Made an effort to involve others by inviting ideas etc	Made no attempt to involve quieter members

How to be successful in Team Assessments

The most important piece of advice I can give you for handling the team assessment well is to relax and enjoy it! Have fun with the task and show your enthusiasm and positive approach to others. Other important behaviours are listed below:

- Listen carefully to and/or read the task briefing and make sure you understand what is required.

- Note the time and how long you have to complete the task.

- Show interest by sitting forward rather than leaning back.

- If you like to lead and want to chair the discussion then do so.

- Listen to others and show you are listening by keeping eye contact, nodding, smiling and agreeing.

- Be aware of what the other members of the group are saying and doing.

- Participate as much as possible without excluding others.

- Build on what others have said rather than just disagreeing with them.

- Be polite, courteous and encouraging to others.

- Keep the discussion on track.

- Put your point of view clearly. Consider counter arguments and be prepared to change your mind.

- Lastly - ignore the observers and enjoy it!

Handling tricky situations

There are some difficulties, which might present themselves in a team assessment - an individual perhaps, who hogs the proceedings, presumably in the mistaken belief that it is wanted. This makes it extremely difficult for quieter members to get a word in edgeways.

However, it is not enough to allow that to happen and to trust the observers to give you the benefit of the doubt in the face of impossible odds. To give them some evidence, you need to employ some strategies to become involved. At the very least you should be showing your interest by agreeing or disagreeing. I know we are all taught that it is not polite to interrupt others, but there are exceptions to this rule and this is definitely one of them!

1. Sit forward, look directly at the person and, with a smile, speak in a clear, firm friendly tone of voice say: "I'm really sorry to have to interrupt you but I would really like to say something here". Say what you want to say and then, still smiling, hand the conversation over, possibly to another quiet member of the team. E.g: "what do you think, Charlotte?"

2. Raising your hand as you speak often helps to get attention too and quite often the difficult person quickly recognizes they have gone too far and calms down. Just like the above example, as soon as you have made your point, pass the discussion directly to another person who has been excluded.

However, if you really do not think you have the confidence to act on either of those suggestions, simply concentrate on your listening skills - the active ones as mentioned above. Remember, the only thing that will guarantee failure is not participating!

The 4th Stage
Your Personal Interview

"I wanted as much information about what sort of questions to expect at the interview so that I could prepare myself mentally. After reading through this section, I was able to formulate answers that demonstrated my experience in the relevant areas and one day after my interview with British Airways, I was offered the position."

Gemma Batchelor
Cabin Crew
British Airways

Personal Interview - 4th Stage

The final stage of a cabin crew interview is the personal interview. So if you reach this point – congratulations. The recruitment team clearly likes what they have seen of you and now need final confirmation that you have the qualities and skills they are looking for.

This is your chance to really shine and show your genuine enthusiasm for the job and interest in the company and the industry as a whole.

Two or more recruitment personnel will use their interview skills to discover a little more about who you are and what makes you tick! They are usually extremely friendly, welcoming and reassuring and will do their best to put you at ease. They want you to have the best possible opportunity to sell yourself well.

It's important for any recruitment team to learn how you approach different situations in the work place, so you will be asked to provide specific examples to the questions they ask.

NOTE: If you have completed a cabin crew application form that has asked you for specific examples, then your interview examples must be different from those on your application form.

They will be looking for you to show the following:

1. Different situations you have been faced with

2. How you dealt with each situation

3. How you felt when you were faced with the situation

4. How the other person involved may have felt during the situation

5. What you learned from the experience.

Questions you can expect to come up at your cabin crew interview are listed on the following pages with some positive indicators, which recruitment teams are expecting from the interviewee, provided as a guideline. The main rule of thumb is to be positive and enthusiastic in all your answers and remember to think from the customer or team's perspective before yours.

Unless stated otherwise, all the questions provided overleaf are typical interview questions that BA and Virgin and many other airline recruitment teams will ask their applicants.

Airline 2-1 Interview Questions and Answers Practice

Interviewer questions	Positive indicators the recruitment team looks for
Why do you want to work for NAME OF AIRLINE	Shows pride in company e.g. makes the appropriate positive comments about company; has clear reasons why they want to work for company; e.g. successful, good image/brand etc. Want to be part of a successful co. Feel that they can contribute towards the continued success.
How would you describe our market product	Knows what type of product airline operates. E.g. scheduled, charter, budget, domestic, international, etc Can describe what passengers receive on board. Is aware of 2/3/4 tier CABIN STRUCTURE – e.g. first class, business class and world traveller cabins.
Why do you want to be a cabin crew member?	Describes positive aspects of the role: eg. Appealing lifestyle; unpredictable work routine; doing something different. Working with different people all the time; welcoming people from all over the world; genuinely enjoy meeting new people. Enjoy working as part of a team to deliver excellence.
How would you define the role of a cabin crew member? (In other words, what do you think you'll be expected to do?)	Is able to describe the primary role of a cabin crew member – e.g. the safety and welfare of passengers during flight. Is able to explain the importance of cabin crew delivering a high standard of customer service; support the company image through professionalism and excellent grooming; Working well as a team
What skills and qualities can you bring to the role of Air Cabin Crew?	Is able to match own skills acquired, to those needed on board. Describes positive and useful qualities that are relevant to the role: Has experience of working in a team; used to delivering a high standard of customer care; friendly, approachable and helpful; trustworthy; reliable; flexible; caring; responsive to customer needs; sensitive, intelligent, supportive, high standard of personal image.

Interviewer questions	Positive indicators the recruitment team looks for
BA ONLY If we were to offer you a position, which qualities would you need to work on?	Focuses positively on own weaknesses and is able to recognize personal areas for development e.g. recognizes the constraints of an aircraft and the need to serve customers well but quickly which may be different to current practice
BA ONLY What challenges do you think you'd face, changing from your current job to a cabin crew member?	Shows a mature and responsible approach to the various challenges e.g. re-location; training etc
BA ONLY What personal development have you achieved during employment? How has it helped you in your job?	Able to describe skills they have gained through previous roles e.g. Able to recognize the value of communicating effectively; understands the importance of excellent service for future customer loyalty; understands that individual needs may require a sensitive approach etc
Please describe in as much detail as possible, a real situation in which you gave excellent customer service. What were the circumstances? What made the service excellent?	Gave a customer service example which demonstrated a personal commitment to delivering excellent customer service. Spoke from the customer's perspective rather than their own. Shows a clear understanding of how their action made the customer feel and the importance of a positive outcome for the customer. Demonstrated a genuine interest, and gave clear examples of how they exceeded customer's expectations. Is able to show that nothing is too much trouble and they are prepared to go the extra mile to ensure customer satisfaction is exceeded.

Interviewer questions	Positive indicators the recruitment team looks for
Please tell us about a time when you have had to deal with an angry customer. Describe how you felt when you were faced with this situation?	Handled situation confidently, showed appropriate company/job knowledge. Saw situation from the customer's perspective and demonstrated appropriate empathy. Owned the problem, listened well, didn't get defensive, looked for realistic solutions and worked hard to achieve these.
Describe a time when you have met/worked with people from another culture. What ways were they different? How did you feel? What did you learn most about that culture?	Shows an enthusiasm to relate to understand and accept other cultures and their respective behaviours e.g. showed a willingness to adapt behaviour to relate best to others. Is prepared to slow down n to allow others to gain better understanding
Describe a time recently when you have had to think quickly on your feet? E.g. What were the circumstances? And how did you manage the situation?	Demonstrated initiative/ ability to take necessary action. Willing to deviate from routine. Adopts a positive, enthusiastic approach to try and rectify situation. Remained business focused.
Describe a time when you have had to /demonstrate flexibility at work or change a routine at work. How did you feel about it?	Demonstrated a flexible, positive approach to changes in routines at work and responds positively. e.g: Speaks positively about the benefits of the change of routine. Tackles the change enthusiastically.

Interviewer questions	Positive indicators the recruitment team looks for
a) Please give an example of when you have been put under pressure at work? What was the situation? How did you deal with it? b) If we were a fly on the wall during this time, what would we see?	Handles personal or work pressure positively – focuses on job in hand. Adopts a positive attitude to reach objectives. Prioritizes well. Helps others or seeks appropriate help to achieve set objectives/time scales etc. Supportive towards team effort
Describe a time when you feel you've involved members of your team	Able to relate an example of motivating and involving all members of team e.g. perhaps called a meeting to find out how other team members feel about particular matters and what they would like to happen for positive results etc.
Tell us about a time when you've experienced a problem or difficulty from another colleague? How did you feel about it at the time and what did you learn from it?	Is not afraid to describe a situation that was an unpleasant experience; is able to focus on the positive aspects of the event and learn from the experience.
Describe a time when you have been unhappy at work (did any of your colleagues pick up on your unhappiness? If so, how did you deal with this situation and what did you learn from it?)	Positive approach to situation – recognizes the impact own behaviour can have on others and works hard to address issues

Interviewer questions	Positive indicators the recruitment team looks for
VIRGIN ONLY Describe a time when you have had a disagreement with a manager at work/been criticized. OR You've had to stand up to a senior staff member?	Able to accept and understand the importance of communicating effectively. Recognizes the importance of NOT becoming defensive or argumentative. Is able to show initiative in ensuring the reason for the criticism is resolved effectively
VIRGIN ONLY If you could be someone famous for the day – who would it be and why?	Demonstrates an enthusiastic/ positive/ fun/ thoughtful/creative/admiring attitude towards the personality traits of famous person and is able to give clear and highly positive reasons why they would like to be that person for the day
VIRGIN ONLY If you were unsuccessful with your application, how would you deal with it? Would you apply again?	Enthusiastic and positive attitude: e.g. " I will reflect on my areas of weakness and do what I can to prepare myself better for the next interview!" etc
VIRGIN ONLY Describe a time when you've used 'Virgin Flair'!	Able to show a fun, spontaneous and thoughtfully different style to surprise and delight their audience – just as Virgin would.
ANY QUESTIONS YOU WOULD LIKE TO ASK US?	Asked at least 2 questions showing interest in our company and in their long term future with us. e.g. asked relative questions about the company's future goals/promotion prospects/personal development opportunities/ how long the new recruit training will be? Etc

Some extra help with your answers

Answers to interview questions

QUESTION: **Why do you want to work for this airline?**

ANSWER: It has an excellent reputation for (quality/low fares/great value / consistency etc) and you are recognized in the aviation world as being leaders in: no frills travel/low fares/a quality brand....

You are successful in what you do and I really like the image that your airline represents: e.g. Quality; Value for money; Modern; Innovative; Caring; Fresh

When people think of (NAME OF AIRLINE) they know what they are getting. Your product is high quality; consistent and reliable and you show that you care about your customers. I would really like to be part of /involved in such an innovative and forward thinking company. I know that I'll be able to contribute towards its future success

NOTE: Airlines ask this question because they want to learn what knowledge you have about them, their product and their business. However, many interviewees make the mistake of responding to this question by stating why they want to become cabin crew member! They should however grab the golden opportunity handed to them to show their enthusiasm about the airline they are applying to.

QUESTION: **Why do you want to be a cabin crew member?**

ANSWER: It's an exciting and happy industry and I want to be part of it! It's been a lifelong ambition of mine to become a cabin crew member.

I have the skills and qualities that will contribute to the standard of customer service passengers expect.

The non routine work pattern really appeals to me; I want to meet and work with a wider range of people; I believe that being a cabin crew member will allow me to develop my customer service and communication skills even further.

I have flown many times myself and I know what a passenger expects from their flight. I would love the opportunity to ensure each passenger has a memorable experience with the airline. I'd love the opportunity to transfer the skills and qualities I have, to a wider audience.

QUESTION: **What business challenges does our airline face as an organisation; and**

How do you think the role of Air Cabin Crew can help address these?

ANSWER: You are currently in competition with: the major airlines/low fare/'no frills' airlines (delete as appropriate).In addition to this, the current rising aviation fuel costs must have a huge financial impact on the business; you also face a continual need to improve/move forward to meet the changing needs and expectations of the traveller. The terrorist threats of the 21st century must present a huge challenge to your airline.

Cabin Crew are the face of the airline and can have a big impact on the image and experience a customer has of the airline. Cabin crew should aim to deliver consistent excellent customer service, e.g. treat each customer as an individual and be prepared to go the extra mile to make each customer feel special and really valued so that they want to come back to your airline again and again.

QUESTION: **Describe a real situation in which you gave excellent service. What was the situation and what made it excellent?**

ANSWER: Recently at work I answered a telephone call from a German doctor who wanted to discuss matters relating to her imminent relocation to the UK. While talking to her I could sense that she was feeling very apprehensive about the relocation as it was her first time to England and she did not know anyone. I could imagine how stressful it might be for her and I tried to think of what I could do to help reduce her worries. When she told me her flight arrival time was at 7.15pm I realized that since her flight would arrive in the evening after work hours, I could go and meet her at the airport and drive her to her new home. I told her my plans and she was ecstatic to know that she wasn't going to be on her own. The day the doctor was arriving, I went directly to the airport after work to meet her and when she came through the arrivals hall at the airport and saw me, the look of relief on her face was very rewarding. I felt really pleased that with just a little extra effort, I had made such a difference to help make someone feel safe and welcomed.

QUESTION: Other than an interest in working with people and flying the world, what skills and qualities can you bring to the role of Air Cabin Crew?

ANSWER: *select the skills and qualities that you feel are strengths of yours*

SKILLS: I am used to working in different teams; I have experience in dealing with customers and I understand the importance of excellent service for future customer loyalty. Having been a passenger many times, I know what a customer expects from their flight and believe that my personal qualities, together with the skills and experience gained over the years will enable me to meet and exceed their expectations.

I am used to working under pressure and to tight time scales and I thrive on the challenges that these situations create. I am also an experienced team player and always work hard to support and contribute well towards the overall team goal for success.

QUALITIES: I am a fun, confident, caring person. I am not afraid of hard work. I love to put a smile on someone's face. When looking after customers or my colleagues, I make sure that I treat each person as an individual and try to show them that they are valued. I am friendly and cheerful and am also a self-motivated person. I take great pride in my personal appearance and would love the chance to wear your smart uniform!

QUESTION: Describe a time when you've been unhappy at work. How did you deal with this?

TIP: *You really must try to give an example – what they are looking for is for a mature and responsible approach to the problem and that if you have been unhappy (for whatever reason) you learned from the experience. E.g. "I learnt that feelings will often show even if you try to hide them, so it's important to try and keep personal problems out of the workplace; (or) it's important to talk to someone about the way you feel - after all, a problem shared is a problem halved"*

QUESTION: Describe a time when you've had to deal with an angry/upset customer? How did you feel? How did you resolve the situation?

TIP: *Use a recent experience and try to keep it work related if possible and at this stage, simply recount the situation, stating the facts only. E.g.*

"I was working as a nurse at hospital. A patient of mine had been refused surgery because she had consumed water prior to the operation. There had obviously been a breakdown of communication and she was understandably angry and very upset. I could imagine she was already feeling very tense about her operation.

I listened to what she had to say and then apologized on behalf of the hospital for the cancelled surgery. When I had managed to calm her down, I was able to explain to her how the cancellation had been for her own protection. I also arranged for the anaesthetist to visit her that morning and a new surgery appointment was made for later that day. The situation was resolved and the patient was happy."

QUESTION: Describe a time or situation in the work place when you've had to be really flexible.

ANSWER: Recently I was on duty at the Andover Hotel and I noticed an elderly couple in the reception area looking rather anxious. They were guests of the hotel. I went over to ask if everything was ok and they explained that they couldn't get down the stairs to the dining room for their meal. Unfortunately the hotel does not have 'lift' access to the dining room. I could see that flexibility was required for this situation and suggested providing them with a restaurant service in the lounge if they would prefer. They were delighted with the proposition. I made sure they were comfortable in the lounge and offered them a drink while I went to get them a menu. I then described the various meals to them and took their order. I moved between the dining room and the lounge regularly to check their requirements were being met and that they were receiving the same level of service that other dining guests were enjoying. At the end of the meal, the elderly couple said that they had been made to feel very special and I was just pleased that I had been able to turn their negative experience into a highly positive and memorable one.

80

QUESTION: Please give an example of when you have felt under pressure at work. What was the situation, how did you deal with it and what was the outcome?

ANSWER: While working for (name of company) I was preparing a presentation for a client meeting. , I had a call from reception informing me that the clients had arrived 2 hours early. This posed 2 problems – one was that I hadn't finished the presentation and the other was that there might not be an available meeting room. Fortunately, I was able to make a phone call to the meeting room people who found me a suitable room and arranged refreshments to keep the clients occupied until I could get the presentation finished.

QUESTION: Please give an example of when you had to work as part of a successful team. What made the team successful? How, as an individual, did you contribute to the team?

ANSWER: *Make sure you answer each part of the question: you'll need to consider a time when you have been part of a successful team. The ideas listed here should guide you*

One team I have been part of and which was successful is the team I am currently working in. Our job as a team is to maximise sales figures, whilst delivering a top quality service. It was a very successful team for many reasons. We enjoyed working together towards a very tight deadline, we pulled together and everyone shared the same goal. We were lucky to have a very good leader, who motivated us all and our team very much became a family unit. We all strived for success and had strong work methods and guidelines to work to. We all knew our individual roles and we took time to share our skills and knowledge with each other. Our team was highly successful because not only did we support each other, but we trusted each other and formed strong friendships and bonds that have lasted to this day. As an individual, I helped achieve success by carrying out my own responsibilities professionally and efficiently. I also believe that I am a good listener and never failed to be there for my team-mates. I enjoy being part of this successful and strong team.

QUESTION: Describe a recent work experience where you have been required to think on your feet in order to resolve a situation that required immediate action. What prompted you to act as you did? How did you resolve it? What was the outcome?

ANSWER: Whilst I was working on reception, a guest at our hotel came to the front desk and complained there weren't any staff available to serve him coffee. He was quite annoyed and agitated, stating that this was the second time he had been kept waiting for a service recently. I apologized to him immediately and told him I would be very happy to serve him. I invited the guest to take a seat in the sitting room and offered him a newspaper while he was waiting. I called the front desk manager to ask if she would cover the reception area while I went to the restaurant to make the coffee. I then brought him his coffee along with some biscuits and informed him that there would be no charge. The guest thanked me for going to such trouble. I was concerned that the level of dissatisfaction could prompt this customer to take his business somewhere else. I believe this action ensured that the customer received the service he was expecting and that he would be happy to use our hotel in the future.

QUESTION: Imagine you are a crewmember onboard a very busy flight. The passenger call bells are going every second and you are rushed off your feet. You notice one of your colleagues sitting on the jump seat, ignoring the call bells and reading a newspaper. How would you deal with this situation?

ANSWER: I would approach the seated crew member cheerfully and say in a tactful way "I'm really busy getting some blankets for passengers in row 32 –so would you mind answering that call bell".

QUESTION: Describe a time when you have involved members of your team?

ANSWER: Use an example that show the recruitment team your ability to people feel 'involved' and that you are able to draw on the skills and knowledge of your team members to help achieve the objective effectively and successfully.

Working with different cultures

Questions on your attitude and flexibility towards different cultures will be tested. What you need to be demonstrating here is your ability to show a sincere interest in people from different cultures and to recognize in a positive enthusiastic way that just because other cultures do things differently from your own culture, it isn't wrong – that we can learn from different cultures.

QUESTION: **Tell us about a time when you have met or worked with a different culture. What was different/ difficult? What did you learn from the experience?**

ANSWER: I recently went on holiday to Honk Kong, where the culture is very different from our own. One thing that impressed me was their passion for making a sale to their customers. They were always so determined to get me to buy and they would use their charm, knowledge and great sales talk! This approach is very different from the British, reserved selling approach and I believe we could learn great things from each other. It would be so nice if just occasionally the same level of passion was evident in the UK!. Who knows, sales for UK may increase as a result of the Chinese way!

QUESTION: **(a) If you are not successful at this interview how would you deal with it?**

(b) Would you re-apply?

ANSWER: (a) I'd be very upset and disappointed naturally! But I would try to remain positive and focused. I won't give up until I am wearing the uniform!!

(b) Definitely! I would reflect on areas that I may have been weak on and try to prepare myself better for the next interview in 6 months time!

Concluding the Interview

Usually you are invited at the end of an interview to ask any questions of your own.

This is your opportunity to show some initiative and imagination. Make sure that you ask AT LEAST TWO questions! It will further demonstrate your enthusiasm and interest in them as a company and your potential employment with them.

Some examples of questions that you could ask are listed below:

1. I'm really interested in the training programme that I would be doing if I am successful. Can you tell me a little bit more about what's involved please?

2. How soon after being successful would I be placed on a training programme?

3. "I am looking for a long term career with you and if I am lucky enough to be offered a position with (NAME OF AIRLINE) what opportunities would there be for promotion in the future?"

4. "Would there be opportunities in the future for me to diversify and move into other areas of the airline?"

5. "What plans does NAME OF AIRLINE have for the future? (e.g. does it want expand its market share/ extend its network/ within (UK/Europe/USA/Far East etc)"

6. "If I were to be offered a position with your airline, I would be very interested in developing my language skills in French/Spanish/Arabic to further develop my skills in customer service - would (name of airline) support this?"

At the end of the interview, give an enthusiastic smile, shake hands firmly again and thank the interviewer(s) for their time. It's always nice to leave with a comment such as "Thank you for giving me an opportunity to meet you. I look forward to hearing from you soon".

Some Useful Notes To Consider When At Your 2 – 1 Interview

Establishing Rapport

Interviewing is based on taking turns. The better you are at listening, the better you will know when to speak and what to say. If you are a naturally talkative person you are going to have to practice your listening skills more often! Don't be tempted to go into too much detail. Just listen carefully to the question and answer as concisely as possible.

If you sense you are failing to establish a rapport don't get despondent, instead quickly evaluate the following points:

1. Have you answered the question that they asked? E.g. consider the following question. "Why do you want to work for First Choice?" This question is giving you an opportunity to sound really enthusiastic about them – and does not ask you to explain that you want to become a cabin crew member etc.

2. Are you talking too much? Pause more often and shorten your answers.

3. Are your answers so short that they sound curt? Soften your tone. Show the interviewer that you are interested by nodding, keeping eye contact and smiling appropriately.

4. Respond with energy. Speak clearly, and use facial expressions as a visual aid to emphasise your meaning.

Tricky Questions

However much you prepare your ideas, you are bound to find yourself facing one or two difficult questions –e.g. those that take you by surprise, or those that you hoped would never be asked. Pause, think and take your time. Whatever you do, don't panic.

Explain to the interviewer that the question asked requires some thought. If you really are stuck, and cannot answer a question, then it is best to say so. A quietly confident admission of ignorance is more impressive than trying to bluff your way through. E.g. "I'm really sorry. I can't answer that one. However I'm really interested in knowing the answer. Would you be able to tell me?"

THE OUTCOME

Many airlines are switching to electronic means of communicating and airlines that are communicating this way (British Airways for instance) will send you an email advising you of the outcome. However, many airlines still adopt the traditional methods by using letter or phone. The general rule of thumb is this:

A large envelope through the door will signify you have been successful – because all the details/contract of employment etc will be inside the envelope!

Perfect People Skills

"Most of what I really need to know about how to live and what to do, and how to be, I learned in nursery school. Wisdom was not at the top of the graduate school mountain, but there in the sandbox at nursery school. These are the things I learned:

Share everything; play fair; don't hit people; put things back where you found them; clean up your own mess; don't take things that aren't yours; say you're sorry when you hurt somebody; wash your hands before you eat..."

Robert Fulghum
Author

People Matter

"Most of the time our people skills are, to borrow a phrase which has passed into the common language of psychology, good enough. However, sometimes good enough is not good enough"

In the world we live in today, it would seem that good people behaviour that was once taken for granted, has unfortunately been downsized and out placed. Good manners seem to have been replaced by selfishness, greed, a lack of respect and a total inability to see things from another persons' perspective. In fact I sometimes think we have made our lives so unnecessarily complicated by forgetting some of the most basic qualities, such as graceful politeness and general courtesy.

These days, people seem unwilling to acknowledge another human being with a simple yet meaningful gesture such as a smile. It's sad because giving someone a smile costs nothing, yet is one of the richest gifts you can bestow on another person.

The purpose of this section is to really remind you of the basic skills which can make the difference between building relationships with people and merely co-existing. It's about things which can really make a difference when you interact with another person. After all, people matter... don't they?

I'd like to think that after reading through the sections on communication, customer service and teamwork skills, you will be encouraged to look at your own people skills more carefully so that you can be more aware of the effect your behaviour can have on others.

Becoming much more in tune with how you look to others and how others perceive you will enable you to demonstrate your perfect people skills and hopefully achieve the success you are seeking at your airline interview. I hope you'll enjoy this little journey back in time!

Communication Skills

"Like everyone else, I believed my communication skills were good. I found this section really interesting and useful to me and now practice better communication skills in my everyday life"

Selena Newton
Cabin Crew
Virgin Atlantic

The Vital Role of Communication

It is your skills in being able to communicate effectively which links all the elements discussed in previous chapters together, and will help you to secure the job of your dreams. Effective communication will also play a crucial part in your role as a cabin crew member.

For that reason, I'd like to examine certain basic elements of the communication process in more detail to see what can work for you effectively and to examine the things you do which can work against you especially at an interview.

In its simplest definition, communication is the giving and receiving of information.   However, effective communication is always a two-way process and works through behaviour.

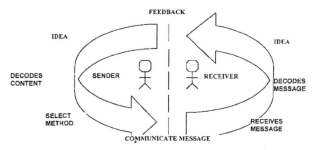

- The sender has an idea;

- The sender decides how to form the idea into a message;

- The sender decides the method of communicating the message;

- The sender sends the message;

- The receiver receives the message;

- The receiver decodes the idea from the message;

- The receiver understands the idea;

- The receiver gives the sender feedback to acknowledge that the message has been received and the idea understood.

The communication process can break down in the following ways

- In the message receiving

- In our decoding mechanism

- In our feedback mechanism

Often, as the sender, we make assumptions about how the receiver is going to decode our message or, as the receiver, we make assumptions about the message that has been sent. As a result of assumptions, our efforts at communication can break down because:

- The message might not be received correctly

- The receiver might not decode the message successfully

- The receiver might decode the message and arrive at a different idea

- The receiver might not give the sender any feedback

It's also useful to remember that without feedback there can never be any guarantee that the original idea has been successfully communicated.

A communication message comprises 3 elements:

1. The Words We Use

2. The Way We Say The Words

3. Our Body Language

Research has shown that the proportion each of these elements contributes to the communication of the message is:

- 7% through the words we use;

- 38% based on the way we say the words (which indicates attitude and feeling etc); and

- 55% through our body language

In other words, your body language is the most influential and powerful form of communication you have. I've already mentioned in previous chapters that what you look like, what you do and the way that you do it makes up more than half the total message – before you have even uttered one word! This is especially true when first impressions are formed. It is the start of how you will be judged and it often affects subsequent communication too.

Remember also that your body language will communicate to an observer, often subconsciously, exactly how you are feeling and what you are really thinking! A good example to draw on here is the 'false smile'.

We know instinctively when a smile is false and the message that we interpret from this non verbal behaviour is that, although they are smiling, their feelings inside have given away the fact that they don't want to smile or that they are not happy.

If there is not a positive thought behind a gesture or greeting, the gesture will feel hollow. You cannot smile at someone and expect it to be received as a genuine smile if all the time you are thinking "my god, what an awful blouse she is wearing!"

So, when looking to improve your personal image or hoping to create a positive first impression, concentrate on your body language first asking yourself "How do I look to others?", "Do I look warm and friendly?", "Do I appear approachable?" and "How enthusiastic do I look and sound?".

Five Steps to Positive Non-Verbal Communication

Body language (55%)

Because your body language has such a huge influence on your communication skills, the last thing you want is for the recruitment team to interpret your body language incorrectly.

There are 5 easy steps that you can take to ensure that your non verbal communication with others is a highly positive one.

1. Eye contact

To begin the communication process effectively your eye contact should be always be courteous and strong. Averting your eyes whilst someone is talking to you is very frustrating and off-putting. Think about how you feel when someone does this to you. Avoiding eye contact with someone, for whatever reason, may cause the person who you are talking with to think one or all of the following:

- This person does not like me
- This person is not listening to what I am saying
- This person considers themselves above me
- This person is shy

So, you must make eye contact with people you are interacting with. Long enough to:

- Acknowledge them as individuals.
- Make yourself appear approachable.
- Show respect towards the person you are communicating with.

In other words, eye contact is essential and not an option!

2. A Smiling Face

Often on meeting a person we look at the face first and make personality and other judgements on the basis of what we see. Be aware that your facial expression often shows your emotions and how you feel. A smile is seen as welcoming; it shows you are friendly. There are some more good reasons for smiling too. Smiling releases natural hormones in our brain, called endorphins, which help make us feel good. Also, when you smile you are always so much more attractive!

3. Posture

How do you feel when you are trying to communicate with someone who has poor posture i.e. slouches; body angled away from you. You may well be thinking they are not that interested in what you have to say or perhaps they can't be bothered to listen, or that they may be bored by you.

Your posture communicates a tremendous amount about you. Good posture reflects the energy and enthusiasm you are feeling and how positive you are.

Stand alert but relaxed, with the back straight and the tummy tucked in. If you are seated, lean forward to show interest.

4. Physical Barriers

Research has proved that as much as 40% of what you are saying may not be heard due to the physical distractions caused by hands/fingers/arm gestures. Your listener will be pre-occupied watching all your movements.

If you normally gesticulate with your hands be aware that you could be causing too much distraction – particularly at an interview. I always make a special effort to keep them clasped together on my lap.

5. Stillness

When we are feeling threatened, nervous or panicky (especially during an interview assessment), we tend to use more gestures and adopt habits like foot tapping, nail biting, smoothing back hair, playing with objects or doodling etc whereas a minimum of movement suggests that you are in control and calm. So, in an effort to be perceived as professional and calm try to control any nervous habits you may have during your interview – even if this means sitting on your hands.

Positive Verbal Communication

How You Say It (38%)

Tone of Voice

How you say what you say, makes up 38% of your communication. Your tone reflects your attitude and your attitude reflects your emotions/feelings and the way that you behave. Have you ever tried to say "hello" in a happy voice without smiling?

When communicating with others use your voice well to reflect sincerity, enthusiasm, pleasantness and confidence which will help to build the necessary rapport that you are seeking during the interaction.

You can further build rapport through your verbal behaviour in the following ways:

- Empathizing
- Asking Questions
- Checking understanding
- Sympathizing
- Making useful/realistic suggestions

Empathy

While I'm on the subject, I'd just like to re-enforce the importance of empathy because it is the single and most effective rapport builder in any verbal communication.

To find out how we affect others and to be aware, generally of what others are think and feeling, the skill we need is empathy. People often confuse empathy and sympathy so let me begin by getting the difference clear.

Sympathy is putting your arm around someone and commiserating with them: "I am so sorry to hear about your cat being run over..."

Empathy is stepping into their shoes and understanding through painstaking listening and questioning, exactly what it is they are feeling, what it is like to be them at this moment.

Sympathy, in its own place and expressed with sincerity, compassion and sensitivity is a vital quality, but being able to sympathize with someone is not a skill in quite the same way as empathizing. For me, empathy means that wonderful gift which some people have of making me feel that I am the most important person in the world, and yet at the same time being sufficiently objective to give me precisely the right advice. That combination of closeness and the clarity which comes with distance is what I aim for when I am trying to empathize.

Empathy is important because it enables us to understand how other people are; what makes them tick, how their worlds work and what really matters to them. It is also empathy, and empathy alone, that will help you to deal with the difficult people you meet in life or handle complaints and problems more effectively. It may not always work, but at least you will have the satisfaction of knowing, if you have used it, that nothing else would work; that you have done your best.

NOTE: When completing your application form, it's always a good idea to provide examples of empathy where ever possible.

The Words You Use (7%)

Although what you say only contributes 7% to the overall message, it is the vital link in communication and it is important to ensure that what you say is matching your body language – remember the false smile!

The problem with words

Have you ever had the feeling that although you have done your best to communicate something in words, somehow there are gaps in what you have said? Or that the full impact of some experience has got lost in the telling? Or that however carefully you have tried to explain something, your listeners have missed the vital point?

There is a real problem with words. However carefully we use them, they are always a representation of what we mean. The weakness of words is that they only provide a one-dimensional tool to convey our three dimensional thoughts, emotions, experiences. Some of us get over the inadequacies of language better than others. The great poets and novelists, for example, become great, precisely because they are able to use language which transcends its own limitations. They have the same black squiggles on the page as the rest of us, and yet they can use them in a way which allows us to see and feel and hear what they describe.

At an airline interview, the words you choose to use are going to have an impact on your listeners so try to ensure they are relevant and appropriate

The words you choose will often help you to check your understanding of what you have just heard and you can do this effectively by repeating back what has just been said, paraphrasing or simply asking questions to clarify what you have heard.

Summary

1. Use Empathy - put yourself in the speaker's shoes and try to see things from their perspective

2. Use Questions – to demonstrate your interest in the speaker

3. When you smile your brain releases endorphins, which makes you feel good.

4. Avoid Interruptions - wherever possible, don't allow yourself to be interrupted from your speaker

The Art of Listening

Definition of a bore:

"A person who talks when you want them to listen"

Ambrose Bierce

I can't leave the subject of communication without mentioning the importance of good listening skills.

Listening is what we all do all the time! We listen to the radio; we listen to the T.V.; we listen to our children, our parents, our bosses, customers, colleagues. We spend our lives listening. Or do we? I don't think we do!

So what are we doing all that time when our ears are open and other people are making noises at us.

I'll tell you what we are doing. We are thinking about what we are going to say when it is our turn to speak. We are wondering what is for lunch. We are remembering something We have to do before the weekend. We are **hearing** what is being said to us, but we are not really paying attention to it.

Because we are not really paying attention, the other person is beginning to feel frustrated and so tries harder. Therefore, they put their point more strongly, which makes us who are supposed to be listening, begin to resent this ear-bashing and concentrate even harder on what we are going to say when we get the chance. Because the person speaking feels that chance approaching, they get even more desperate to …you get the drift.

So why is listening and paying attention to people, such a challenge? Perhaps it is because we are so bombarded by noise and distraction these days that we unconsciously filter out most of what comes at us. Our modern terror of silence means that we are losing the discipline and skill of giving our full attention to others.

WHY LISTENING IS IMPORTANT?

Because few people really feel listened to these days, they seek other ways of getting attention. Kids scrawl on walls; adults get drunk and managers spread rumour and innuendos.

There is something good which comes out of the lack of real listening. It means that when you do listen, I mean, *really* listen, to someone, the experience will be so novel and so special for them, you will have a friend for life! This tells you how important it is for people to *feel* that they have been listened to.

When people are listened to they feel they *matter*, that what they think and feel is important; that they are important. When people feel important (not over important though, because that leads to a whole other set of problems: but important enough to warrant attention) they feel responsible and they act responsibly. This is why listening is important.

It is also important for a number of more prosaic and less drastic reasons:

- **Listening solves mutual problems:** it is ridiculous to disagree with someone until you understand their point of view.

- **Listening leads to co-operation:** when people reckon they are important to you they will be more inclined to respect you in return and co-operate with you.

- **Listening helps your decision-making:** by listening to the experience and ideas of others you improve your own judgement.

- **Listening builds your own confidence:** the more you understand others, the more likely you re to do and say things to which they will respond positively.

- **Listening prevents conflict:** talking before listening leads to the foot-in-the-mouth experiences we never forget. You have two ears and one mouth: take the hint!

HOW TO LISTEN PROPERLY

The skills I am about to describe go under the general banner heading of *active listening*. Active rather than passive, I suppose, though I would prefer to think that proper listening can only be active listening.

There are four foundations of active listening: think of this as the RASE process for **raising** the quality of your listening skills!

1. R – RESPONDING TO THE CONTENT (the subject matter of what is being said)

2. A – ACKNOWLEDGING THE FEELINGS (underlying what is said)

3. S – SHOWING YOU UNDERSTAND and accept what is said

4. E – ENCOURAGING FURTHER DISCLOSURE

Let's look at these in turn.

1. Responding to the content

The way you do this is by *paraphrasing* the content. Focus on the main subject of what is being said, and feed it back to the speaker. For example, someone says:

"The atmosphere at work is getting more difficult each day"

Your paraphrased response could be:

"So the situation is getting increasingly serious then"

This simple re-statement tells the speaker you have understood the main point and that you support their perception of the situation. Note that you are only supporting their perception because this is not about judging whether they are right or wrong.

2. Acknowledging the feelings

Then you need to change your focus to the feelings behind what has been said:

"It sounds as if you are feeling very uncomfortable about what is going on"

Acknowledging the emotional content of what is said – even if 'uncomfortable' is not quite the right word – lets them know their feelings are important and are being heard and understood.

3. Showing you understand

This next step is to accept the legitimacy of those feelings, even if you do not agree with them:

> "I can see how much you dislike working in the office when there is so much tension in the air"

The empathy that is used here is important to demonstrate to the speaker that you do understand their feelings, and are not simply just agreeing with them.

4. Encouraging further disclosure

This is the final step in the RASE sequence and this is where you encourage the person to tell you more by asking an open question:

> "What is specifically going on in the office?"

With questions you are now going for detail: I find that word 'specifically' one of the most useful in the language because, until you know something specifically, you don't really know anything.

Now before you get carried away and think these four steps are the key to making friends and jazzing up for life, please do not think that listening begins and ends here. These are merely the foundations. Nor should you start to show off how well you listen – because if you overdo these it will seem strained and unnatural to the speaker – these tools have to be used with delicacy and, more importantly, real sincerity. Fake sincerity provides the cringe factor in many communications we have with others.

MORE ACTIVE LISTENING SKILLS

So those are the foundations of proper listening, but there are lots more for you to practice. Next time you listen to someone- I mean, really listen, try to do the following:

- **Shut up:** You cannot listen and talk at the same time (and this is the hardest skill of all for some people to master)

- **Be patient:** Your gift of time and attention may be the most precious you ever make

- **Concentrate:** Do not let your mind wander off on its own when the speaker says the same thing for the hundredth time. The content may be the same – but the small shifts in tone often tell you as much as the actual words

- **Leave your own feelings behind:** Please do not say "I know how you feel" because in most situations you cannot know how another person feels

- **Look at the speaker:** their posture and gestures will tell you as much about how they feel as what they say. You will also notice if what they are saying is not matched by what their body is telling you. It is the unconscious body movements which will be telling the truth

- **Make eye contact:** Do not stare

- **Don't argue:** either mentally or directly. You may want to put across some different ideas but leave this until you have finished listening and then ask questions

- **Listen for their personality:** The more you can listen and discover about people personally, their likes and dislikes, motivations, ambitions and values, the better you can respond to them

- **Question your own assumptions:** Avoid making instant judgements based on whether you like their hairstyle or their taste in clothes or putting them into boxes and stereotypes based on class, race or gender. Be aware of your own prejudices and how they may interfere with your listening.

Summary

Listening properly can be quite hard work, but when done well is highly rewarding. To be an effective communicator it is important that you look critically at your own abilities and decide what your strengths and weaknesses are in the whole communication process.

Hopefully after reading through this section of the book you are a little more aware of your communication and listening skills and are encouraged to put into practise some of the ideas that have been discussed in order to help you to communicate more effectively for success at your cabin crew interview.

Effective Teams

"The high standard of training I received ensured that my team work and customer service skills would be set apart from the rest at an airline interview. It worked! I was successful. Can't believe I'll be in Bahrain in less than 6 weeks!"

Sarah Eddy
Cabin Crew
Gulf Air

What makes a Team Successful

At an airline interview you will need to stand out from the crowd in your skills as a team player and each applicant is given the opportunity to demonstrate their strong team skills when participating in stage 3 of the interview process, the team assessment. If you pass the team assessment and get put through to stage 4, the personal interview, the interviewers will be asking you lots of questions on how you would cope with different situations that you could face when working in a team. The following chapter will provide you with the latest thinking from business analysts and the teamwork model that airlines follow.

I am sure that you have experience of working in teams of people. You may have wondered why some teams you have worked in have worked really well and produced good results and why some teams you have come across have not been successful and you have not enjoyed being in. This section will help you to pinpoint why.

THE FOUR CIRCLES

There is much written about the many characteristics that make up a successful team, most of which can be broken down into four categories or elements, known as the Four Circles. The main area to concentrate on for your interview is your knowledge and understanding of these important components and being able to relate these well with any examples you provide the recruitment team.

WORK METHODS

In the same way that games of sport need rules, orchestras need sheet music, society needs laws and drivers need a highway code, teams need to have agreed systems of working together – e.g. procedures, rules, methods, and paperwork.

These work methods, if well thought out, serve not to stifle a group, but to give it framework within which it can operate smoothly and efficiently – provided that the other three elements of teamwork are in operation!

One work method which teams need in order to undertake tasks/projects or solve problems together is a systematic process, i.e. step-by-step recipe to guide them through the task in hand.

Teams often benefit from having additional proven work methods for handling and developing ideas, for making decisions, for processing information etc. Elements that are present in WORK METHODS are shown below:

Decision Making	Timekeeping
Work plan	Objectives
Agendas	Standards / rules
Guidelines / briefings	An appointed leader

LEADERSHIP AND CONTROL

It is unlikely that a team will operate successfully without leadership and control unless it primarily repeats the same process, e.g. an orchestra or band playing the same musical repertoire. Often, teams that come together without any nominated leader try to operate without one on a democratic basis. To operate successfully in this way usually requires a very high level of team skills and climate which are not normally present until the team has learned to work well together over a period of time. A leaderless team often procrastinates, gets bogged down, and takes a long time reaching decisions – which are often compromises to keep every one happy!

The leadership role can and does take many different forms; the skills and role of a team leader is a major topic in its own right. Primarily, the role of the leader is to provide the 'right amount' of direction and support to enable the team to perform effectively in achieving its objectives. Typical characteristics of a good Leadership are as follows:

Mediating	Listening
Building on ideas	Gathering information
Checking understanding	Refocusing
Persuading	Directing
Summarising / recapping	Testing understanding

The amount and type of leadership will depend on the ability and willingness of the team members to work together effectively. A leader's role ideally is to orchestrate and co-ordinate the team effort, rather than provide most of the direction for the team to follow. To be able to lead in this way requires effective work methods and an appropriate level and blend of technical and team skills.

The responsibility for leadership and control may well change hands at different stages in a task and may in fact be delegated by the team's formally recognised leader. For example, person A may chair a planning discussion, person B may organise the team, and person C may supervise the implementation; further control may be contributed by a timekeeper.

SKILLS AND KNOWLEDGE

It has been proved that a team needs an appropriate blend of TEAMSKILLS, as well as technical skills, to work together effectively.

Often, the key reason for operating in a team is because no one person has the requisite knowledge, skills and experience to tackle the task alone, profitably or productively. Usually, membership of a work group is based primarily on the technical or functional skills required to do the task. However, the right combination of ingredient skills and knowledge is no guarantee of achievement. Although this depends significantly on the presence of the other three elements, it also depends on team members having other skills in addition to their functional or technical ones. These are probably best referred to as TEAMSKILLS; these include Interpersonal Skills i.e. the skills of interacting with other people effectively – such skills as listening, influencing, handling conflict, motivating etc.

Just as individuals in a team have specialist, technical or functional skills, it is likely that they will also (primarily because of their differences in personality and temperament) have individual TEAMSKILLS to contribute – for example the ability to think creatively, to spot the flaws in others' ideas, a concern for detail and accuracy, a concern for timekeeping or an ability to organize etc. Some key characteristics of Skills and Knowledge are below:

Listening	Decision making
Supporting	Creating ideas
Challenging	Note taking
Differing	Time-keeping

CLIMATE

This element is often overlooked by many teams, possibly because it is less tangible. However, it is the element most frequently cited when people refer to effective teams that they have worked in. A good climate is the product of many things including, though not exclusively, the other three elements – work methods, skills and knowledge, leadership and control.

Climate is also the result of the depth and quality of relationships formed between team members, e.g. the levels of openness, honesty, candour and trust. Climate is also significantly affected by the extent to which each individual member understands values and enjoys working with his fellow team members and the extent to which he feels this is reciprocated. Characteristics that are present in CLIMATE are as follows:

Making mistakes	Trust
Honesty	Openness
Humour	Stating feelings
Self disclosure	Friendship

SUMMARY

These four elements of teamwork are highly inter-related. If any one element is missing, the team's performance is likely to suffer. This can be compared to the performance of a car in which the compression of one cylinder is poor in relation to the other three. The car's performance will be affected – it does not run smoothly, fuel and energy is wasted, it is slower and, if not corrected in time, will soon affect other parts of the engine that will wear out that much quicker.

Best Personal Service

I particularly liked the customer service training because this training would help in any work situation"

Jana Prackova
Cabin Crew
British Airways

Best Personal Service

How many of the following scenarios have you experienced? There are those people who make you wait in front of an empty counter while the staff just gossip among themselves. There are those people who hear phones ringing but don't answer them because it is their lunch hour. Those who take three weeks to reply or who simply never reply at all and there are those people who never smile or make promises that they have no intention of keeping. Worst of all, there are those who believe that if the customer complains, there must be something wrong – with the customer! Overall, these people cheerfully make their customers put up with behaviour which they would never tolerate if it happened to them!!

Are any of those situations familiar? The startling reality is that your overall impression of the company can be coloured because of one individual!

Why Customer Care matters

It costs an airline almost five times more money to win a new customer than to keep existing an one, so airlines are continually striving to retain customer loyalty.

Cabin crew are the face of the airline and have a huge impact on the experience that their customers have. Whilst onboard products can be quickly rivalled, it is the personal service given that becomes unique to that airline. In today's highly aggressive and competitive business, airlines simply cannot afford to recruit people who don't have a genuine passion for delivering excellent customer service.

Best Personal Service is provided by people who establish caring, non-threatening relationships; people who genuinely care about others. Caring about others shows that you have an understanding of their needs and what makes them tick. At an airline interview you will be expected to demonstrate your ability and passion in providing your very best personal service to ensure your customers have a very memorable and highly positive experience.

A definition of Good Service is: Providing the customer with what they want, when they want it, in a friendly and courteous manner.

A definition of Best Personal Service is: Good Service PLUS, being prepared to put self out for others, go the extra mile, show nothing is too much trouble, being creative and anticipating customer needs even before the customer themselves know what it is they need.

Practice giving your Best Personal Service in everyday work situations!

"Since doing the course, my confidence in dealing with customer complaints has grown and now, rather than dreading having to handle an angry customer, I see it as a positive challenge. The techniques I was shown on the course through practical role plays really does work and all my mates come to me now when they have a complaint to deal with"

Kim Wilde
Cabin Crew
Gulf Air

Handling Customer Complaints Successfully!

How good are you at handling customer problems effectively?

As a nation we still tend to view complaints in a negative way. However, it is important to remember that in today's world, customers have higher and higher expectations than ever before and expect their complaint to be handled quickly and effectively.

When a customer complains to a company, it is an effective form of feedback and so should be seen as a positive thing. If you think about it objectively, rather than defensively, customers are letting us know where we are going wrong and giving us the opportunity to put things right.

At an airline interview the recruitment team will be keen to determine how you handle customer problems and grievances and will ask you to describe in detail how you manage the situation, what you are thinking and feeling about the situation and how committed you are to achieving a successful outcome. They want you to provide evidence that you can and do approach customer complaints and/or problems in a positive and objective way that achieves a 'win-win' outcome for all concerned.

The following pages outline the correct approach, attitude and handling of customers when things go wrong for the customer. It is the approach that all airlines will expect you to demonstrate.

Handling customer complaints effectively

Sometimes, even after years of dealing with customer complaints, it's still a shock and can take you "unawares" when someone has a "real go" at you. However, rather than taking it as a personal criticism or getting defensive about the situation which is what many customer service providers do, you need to think about how you are going to deal with the customer's anger and emotion and do whatever you can to diffuse it.

Even though many times it may not be your direct responsibility or your companies fault, as the front line staff member you are the person a customer may complain to.

If a customer has a problem, you need to try and correct it and even if you cannot correct the problem, you should in the very least, ensure that the customer feels confident that you have:

1. Demonstrated an understanding of the effects the problem is having on them

2. You have done all that you can to try to help them.

The biggest rule you must adhere to is to bear in mind that whatever problems your company is experiencing, the customer is not concerned with, nor should they be bothered with, details that are managerial or business related, such as staff shortage, computer breakdown or busy periods.

As unreasonable as it might seem, if the customer has a problem, they won't care whether your building is burning down or you have an emergency of any kind. They want their problem sorted out - immediately.

Think about the last time you had to make a complaint. Apart from the corrective action, what else did you expect the person handling your complaint to do? Your customers will expect the same:

- They want to Be Heard
- They want to Be Understood
- The want to Be Respected
- They want An Apology
- They want An Explanation
- They want Corrective Action As Soon As Possible

As a customer service staff member you should be able to meet at least 5 of those 6 expectations. The only one you may not be able to meet is providing any corrective action because this may be outside your control.

It's important that you are able to put yourself in the customer's position. Try to imagine how they are feeling and remember that you are seen to be the expert, the Ambassador for your company. It's the empathy thing again!

It's also useful to think how you felt when you last made a complaint. Do not judge whether they have a valid complaint or not. It's the customer's perception of their experience that is at issue here.

Why customers become angry

We can become angry when our idealized version of how things should have happened is not realized. As a result, we feel very helpless and sometimes try to intimidate or manipulate the person in charge of our problem. We'll often exaggerate a point or ask for the sun, moon and the stars in order to get what we feel we have been short changed on.

Bring the customer's anger down

If a customer comes to you in your shop, restaurant, hotel, or perhaps calls you on the telephone with a complaint and are very angry, it is often very difficult to reason with that customer because their 'wants' may be very high.

The first thing to do is to deal with the anger because it's very difficult to offer a solution to a person who is angry. When anger is high, reason is low. You may, through personal experience, know that it's almost impossible to be reasonable and rational with someone who is being unreasonable and totally irrational.

Therefore in order to solve the problem you must try to bring the other individual's anger level down to a point where emotions are no longer in the way. I have listed 5 easy steps below that really do work:

How to diffuse anger:

1. Listen

Never ever interrupt or interject until the customer has finished. Customers want to have their say, and you need to let them have it. The speaker you do not interrupt will eventually calm down if not only because of emotional exhaustion.

Once you have listened, let the customer know that you have listened correctly by clarifying and verifying what you have heard. This can be done by re-stating what the customer has said, in your own words.

2. Agree

This is the most effective technique because it is very hard to be disagreeable when someone is agreeing with you! The difficult part is listening to what is being said and then finding something you can agree with. There are two ways to do this:

In Fact: You can agree in fact. If what the customer is telling you is fact, denying it is useless.

"You're right Miss Jones, you requested wheelchair assistance when you booked your ticket with us, and you didn't get it, you have every right to be upset"

In Principle: This is agreeing with the emotions and the feelings that the customer may have experienced. When agreeing in principle, you are not taking the blame or ownership.

"I agree Mrs Jones, it would be frustrating not to have received the information you requested about your onward flight"

Expressions like 'I agree' and 'You're right' are very useful in these situations.

3. Apologize

Customers expect an apology and must always be given one. The trick is to apologize without accepting blame. Remain calm and respectful. Make the apology sincere and appropriate,

4. Remain calm and respectful

Being in the front line delivering customer service is ranked as the fourth most stressful job, after Air Traffic Controllers; Inner City Teachers and the Police!

Let's accept the fact that diffusing anger can be stressful and proceed with understanding some steps to overcome it. It is important to remember that the customer is rarely angry with you personally. It's the situation that has made them angry.

5. Acknowledge the anger

Never ignore the emotional level of the person you are trying to help.

Accept the fact that the customer is angry and acknowledge the feelings and the reasons behind it. Accepting the anger makes it easier to handle and therefore diffuse. Remember it is not you they are angry with – it is what has happened. So don't get defensive, don't take it personally and do everything you can to show that person you understand the problem from their perspective and that you will do everything possible to put it right.

If you follow these 5 steps to reduce a customer's anger when they have a complaint, you will reduce their anger to a more rational level and will then be in a strong position to gain that important WIN -WIN situation.

Throughout your handling of any customer problem or complaint, you'll always have a much higher chance of a positive outcome if you are communicating effectively. This means ensuring your non-verbal behaviours are open and approachable; you are listening well to the customer and your verbal communication matches your body language i.e. you are giving good direct eye contact, your empathy is present and the tone of your voice is non-aggressive and non-defensive.

SOME DON'TS!

What you should never do when trying to reduce a customer's anger level

1. Don't debate the facts. When a customer is angry, they aren't always thinking factually. Emotion and exaggeration may be used in order to get their point across. e.g.: "I never get put through to the person I want to speak to"

2. Don't ask 'why?' questions. E.g. "Why didn't you ask if you didn't understand the terms and conditions"? Asking 'Why?' however nicely implies blame and indicates that you think the customer is wrong.

3. Don't focus on what can't be done. Focus on how you can help the customer. Look for ways that you can pacify the customer, something, which is acceptable to them without focusing on the negative aspects.

4. Don't blame others or pass the buck. Take ownership of the problem and deal with it in a responsible way. It is important for your customer's retention that you handle any complaints you have, sensitively and efficiently. You must reduce the anger levels before you try to solve the problem because when anger is low, reason is high.

To put all this advice into practice just follow the 8A's on the next page. Try to familiarize yourself with this model and put it into practice now. This will give you more confidence to refer to it when describing your customer service situations to the interviewers.

The 8 A's to Handling Complaints

1. **Active Listening.** Don't interrupt; Enquire; Stay on Target; Allow customer to talk through problem; Give good eye contact; Nod your head; Look interested; Repeat back what the customer has just told you.

2. **Apologize, Empathise/Appreciate.** *"I'm really sorry that this has happened Mr Smith. If you have reserved a room and it isn't ready for you, I can understand why you are so upset"* By empathising with the customer, they will recognise that you are seeing the problem from their perspective   Own the problem, don't pass the buck or the blame and don't be dismissive - e.g. *"oh this does sometimes happen!"* or *"we are short staffed at the moment"*

3. **Ask Questions.** Fact find, probe for the real problem; Remain calm, controlled. (keep your body language still) Do not be rude or sarcastic; don't get defensive or emotional.

4. **Alternatives.** Seek alternatives, making sure they are appropriate, realistic. Have a problem solving approach. *"Would you like me take your bags to your room? Would you like to have a drink while you are waiting – compliments of our hotel?"*

5. **Agreement.** Make sure that you get the customer's agreement on what you have offered. Check solution is acceptable. Seek common ground

6. **Action.** You have found out what you can do – so do it!

7. **Aftercare.** Try to go the extra mile! Offer additional suggestions to your customer rather than the bare minimum. Where appropriate, keep your customer informed of your actions. E.g. *"My name is Linda and I am the hotel manager. I will take responsibility to ensure that your room will be ready for you in 20 minutes Mr Smith. Meanwhile, please accept a complimentary bottle of wine to welcome you and your family to our hotel. If you have any future requirements please ask for me and I will be happy to deal with these personally"*

8. **Apology.** Don't forget to seal the transaction with a final apology. E.g. *"Once again, I am sorry about what has happened Mr Smith and I do hope that you enjoy the rest of your stay with us"*. A final apology is what customers expect and will leave them with a lasting impression.

The next time you are called upon to deal with a customer complaint use the 8A's! You'll be amazed at the positive results: a much happier customer; continued business for your company and a rewarding and satisfying experience for you, the service deliverer.

A final note...

A final note...

Being successful at your cabin crew interview relies strongly on having a good blend of both confidence and ability. You'll need to believe in yourself and in the natural good qualities you possess and you'll need to be able to demonstrate your ability in a positive and illustrative way.

However, attempting any difficult task nearly always creates nerves and tension and your own self doubt is the biggest enemy of all to deal with. It is at times when you doubt yourself that you will possibly question your own ability and thereby reduce your own sense of self esteem

Keeping your Self-esteem intact

Self doubt forces you to tell yourself negative thoughts; you end up saying things like:

- I'm not good enough
- I'm bound to fail
- I can't do it

Tasks are always much easier when you are feeling confident, enthusiastic and ready to take action.

Try to put all your nervous energy and adrenalin, to positive use because as soon as you begin to doubt your ability in anything; you are chipping away at your own self-esteem and well being.

Negative thoughts can be easily counteracted by positive thoughts. So start telling yourself positive thoughts: Thoughts such as:

- I'm more than good enough!
- I will succeed!
- I can do it!

This is a highly effective way of building your own confidence and enthusiasm, which will encourage you to take action.

In fact it works so well that sports people are following the Americans' lead in this country and focusing on the power of positive thought as well as physical training.

As soon as you hear that critical thought in your head, turn it around to how you would like it to be. Repeat the new supportive thought often and it should lift you on an upward spiral.

Of course you will have to take practical steps to help you succeed but the supportive thoughts will assist you.

1. Appreciate Your Own Qualities

Stop criticising yourself or overloading on guilt especially when you've made a mistake or don't feel you live up to others expectations. Criticizing yourself only freezes you into inaction and negative thoughts. It is OK to feel angry with yourself but then you have to move on.

2. Think Some New Thoughts

You have had a lifetime of thinking a certain way, believing unjust things that may have been said about you. Perhaps now is the time to think new thoughts?

Who knows your true capabilities? Only you have the power to unlock your true potential. Do not give in to other people and allow them to mould you by criticising or making judgements. Do they really know any better than you? They may think they are right, but you have a different view.

3. Do Not Compare Yourself With Other People

Do not be distracted by comparing yourself to other people. This only undermines your confidence. You are unique with a wealth of qualities that you may not have begun to realize exist.

If you try to be like someone else you will become a carbon copy of them!

4. Be Supportive Of Yourself

Be supportive of yourself especially when you have just made a mistake or are feeling fearful.   We say things to ourselves like:

"I'm so stupid. I bet they think I'm really dreadful! "I don't know how I could have done that. It was really awful." "I'll never forgive myself".

Of course you must feel your feelings but eventually you have to call a halt in order to move on and build yourself up again. So say positive things to yourself like:

"That was silly but I can learn from the experience".

5. Accept Yourself As You Are Now

You have to truly accept yourself as you are now before you can move on to affect a change. If you know that you are not a very punctual person, then it's only you that can make the necessary changes. Accepting yourself for who you are will not make you complacent but will give you the freedom to make the changes you want.

These then, are ways in which we can help to maintain a high sense of self esteem. Of course, as mentioned earlier, positive thoughts alone won't help you to be successful and you'll always need to take the practical steps to support your positive thoughts.

However, if you do your airline research, concentrate on being an effective communicator by becoming more aware of how you look to others, and how others may perceive you and work harder to be a more active listener, you will be demonstrating all the key skills and qualities that an airline recruitment team looks for in potential crew – and success will come your way, naturally.

Good luck!

Test Answers

Test Answers

General Knowledge (from page 49)

1. 1200 hours
2. British Broadcasting Corporation
3. VS
4. Baht
5. 25 (as at Nov 2004)
6. Malta
7. Britannia Airways
8. Railway, Ferry, Eurostar, Coach
9. British Airways
10. November
11. 200 cigarettes
12. Safety Officer
13. Mt Everest
14. Wellington
15. 50 states
16. Any Islamic or Arabic country
17. Universal Co-ordinated Time
18. Independence Day
19. Using the clock method – or – describing where food is on plate
20. Kilimanjaro
21. Heathrow
22. 4
23. North Terminal and South Terminal
24. Airport train service
25. 2
26. British Airports Authority

27. Air Traffic Control

28. Euro

29. 4

30. Criminal record Bureau checks. Security checks. Minimum 5 years employment history check

Addition	Subtraction	Multiplication	Division
1) 36	1) 8	1) 72	1) 11.00
2) 656	2) 24	2) 512	2) 20.00
3) 1542	3) 330	3) 161	3) 108.50
4) 50	4) 413	4) 135	4) 652.43
5) 1861	5) 167	5) 3480	5) 68.25
6) 100696	6) 56988	6) 18728	6) 130.18

Maths Answers (from page 51)

Answers to currency problems on page 52

1. £1.00

2. £3.08

3. $200 is worth £111.11 and he needs to pay £94.00

4. 133 Ringgitt

5. £19.00

6. £104.11

Airline Details

Airline Contact Details

Additional information on popular airlines

Air Atlanta

Website:	www.airatlanta.com
Min.Requirements: Education:	High-school degree/ Matriculation Examination or an equivalent degree.
Minimum Age:	22
Languages:	Speak English fluently plus one additional language, other than any of the common Nordic languages. (Icelandic, Norwegian, Swedish and Danish.)
Other:	Cabin crew Recruitment usually takes place between November – May Contracts offered to successful applicants are normally only temporary as the work is very seasonal, usually finishing in October.
How to apply	Visit website and complete On-line application

bmi

Website:	www.flybmi.com
Min requirements:	
Age:	18-65
Height / Weight	Between 5'2" and 6'.2" in height with weight in proportion. There may be a lower height restriction at some bases where the aircraft type operated has a maximum height allowance of 5'10".
Education:	Minimum 4 GCSE's at grades A – C including English and Maths or the equivalent (NVQ level 2/grade 1 CSE only). Certificates must be presented at interview or before employment
Passport:	Applicants must hold a 10 year British or European passport before employment OR have the indefinite right to live and work in the UK, as well as any relevant visas. Copies of passport stamps should be included with applications from non-European passport holders
Customer Service:	a minimum of 12 month's experience in a customer-facing role
Medical:	a high standard of physical fitness and a visual acuity of 6/9 in each eye, aided or unaided. Contact lenses are preferred but glasses are acceptable
Language:	a good standard of fluency in the English language. A second language is desirable
Image:	immaculate appearance
Desirables:	catering/hospitality knowledge/experience nursing or first aid
HOW TO APPLY	Visit their website (above) for address and then Send a covering letter with current C.V.

Britannia Airways

Website	www.britanniaairways.com
Minimum requirements	
Age:	minimum age is 19
Height / Weight	between 5'2" and 6'.2" in height with weight in proportion
Education:	qualifications: minimum 4 GCSE's at grades A – C including English and Maths or the equivalent (NVQ level 2/grade 1 CSE only). Certificates must be presented at interview or before employment
Passport:	applicants must hold a 10 year British or European passport before employment OR have the indefinite right to live and work in the UK, as well as any relevant visas. Copies of passport stamps should be included with
Customer Service:	a minimum of 12 month's experience in a customer-facing role
Medical:	a high standard of physical fitness
Language:	a good standard of fluency in the English language
HOW TO APPLY	Visit website and complete an on-line application

British Airways

Website:	www.britishairwaysjobs.com
Minimum Requirements:	
Age	Between 19 and 54 at time of application.
Height / Weight:	To be a minimum of 5ft 2in [1.58 metres] in height, with weight in proportion Weight must be of such proportion that the ability to perform all job functions is not hindered.
Education:	GCSE or equivalent standard, with passes in Maths and English. Fluent in English, both written and spoken.
Medical:	A high standard of physical fitness. Complete and successfully pass a medical questionnaire. Satisfy current BA/CAA health requirements.
Passport:	Hold a valid E.U. Passport allowing unrestricted world-wide travel and the right to live and work within the E.U. with no time restrictions.
Location:	Live within 45 minutes of the airport from which you are based.
Additional:	One of the following: • A GNVQ or equivalent qualification in Nursing / Hospitality/ Travel & Tourism or Care Services plus 12 months customer service experience. • 2 years customer service experience.
How to apply	Visit website and complete an on-line application form

City Express

Website:	www.bacitiexpressjobs.com
Minimum Requirements:	
Education:	Educated to GCSE standard or equivalent with passes in English and maths (grade C or above)
Minimum Age:	Aged 18 + at the time of your application
Languages:	
Height:	Between 5'2" (1.58m) and 5'10" (1.77m)
Passport:	Hold a valid EU Passport with the right to live and work in the UK unrestricted and travel worldwide without restrictions
Location:	Able to report for work at your airport base within one hour of call-out
Customer Service:	You'll need 12 months' unbroken customer service experience. It may have been gained in a call centre, or a hotel, or anywhere the focus is on looking after people.
Other:	If you do not have 12 months previous Cabin Crew or Airline Customer Service experience, you are also required to send photocopies of your Maths and English certificates with your application form. Failure to enclose copies with your application will result in a delay to the processing of your application
How to apply	Visit website and download Application Form, Reference Agreement Form and Equal opportunities Form, complete it and send it to the address at the end of the form. Alternatively, please call our Recruitment Hotline on 0161 436 8182

Emirates

Website:	www.emiratesairline.com
Minimum Requirements:	
Education:	Educated to at least high school standard
Minimum Age:	Minimum age 21 years at the time of application.
Languages:	Fluent in written and spoken English (fluency in another language is an asset)
Height:	Minimum arm reach of 212 cms (on tip toes), which will enable you to reach emergency equipment on all aircraft types.
Medical:	Medically fit to meet aircrew requirements.
Customer Service:	Previous experience in the service/ hospitality industry is an advantage. You will be the sort of person who has the natural ability to provide excellent service within a team environment
Other:	If you are successful, you will be located in Dubai, the most modern and cosmopolitan of the Gulf cities, which is becoming renowned for its high-class tourist facilities and its high standard of living.
How to apply	1.Visit website and complete on-line application 2. Visit website for details of open assessment days

easyJet

Website:	www.easyjet.com
Minimum Requirements:	
Education:	A minimum of a C grade average at GCSE level (or equivalent)
Minimum Age:	Aged 18 or over
Languages:	Fluent in spoken and written English
Height / Weight:	Height 5'2" (1.58m) to 6'3" (1.90m) with weight in proportion to height
Medical:	Physically fit
Customer Service:	In possession of at least six months face-to-face customer service experience
Swimming:	Able to swim at least 25 metres
Passport:	In possession of the right to work in the UK and travel freely in the EU
How to apply	Visit their website and complete an on-line application

Excel Airways

Website:	www.xl.com
Minimum Requirements:	
Education:	Minimum 4 GCSE's at grades A – C including English and Maths or the equivalent (NVQ level 2/grade 1 CSE only). Certificates must be presented at interview or before employment
Minimum Age:	Age 18 years – no maximum limit although retirement age is 65 years
Languages:	a good standard of fluency in the English language
Height / Weight:	between 5'2" and 6'.2" in height with weight in proportion
Passport:	Applicants must hold a 10 year British or European passport before employment OR have the indefinite right to live and work in the UK, as well as any relevant visas. Copies of passport stamps should be included with applications from non-European passport holders
Customer Service:	a minimum of 12 month's experience in a customer-facing role
Medical:	a high standard of physical fitness and a visual acuity of 6/9 in each eye, aided or unaided. Contact lenses are preferred but glasses are acceptable
Image:	immaculate appearance
How to apply	Visit website and complete on-line application

First Choice

Website:	www.firstchoice.co.uk
Minimum Requirements:	
Education:	educated to GCSE level
Minimum Age:	20 years of age and over
Languages:	foreign languages are a definite plus
Height;	at least 1.58 metres tall
Swimming:	able to swim 25 metres
Customer Service:	previous experience working with the public is a definite plus
Passport:	Must be entitled to live and work indefinitely in the UK and hold a valid EU or UK passport which permits worldwide travel without restrictions.
How to apply	Visit website and complete on-line application
	Alternatively you can phone 0870 750 1204 and a member of the recruitment team will answer your queries.

FlyBE

Website:	www.flybe.com
Minimum Requirements:	
Education:	3 GCSE passes at Grade C to include Maths and English
Minimum Age:	Minimum 19 years old
Height:	Minimum of 5ft 2in (157cm), maximum 6ft (183cm).
Image:	Neat, presentable appearance with the ability to wear the company uniform is essential. Well cared for hands and nails are also important.
Medical:	Excellent health and hearing. Good eyesight
Passport:	You must be in possession of a full, valid EU passport or ID with no restrictions on your employment in the base of application, nor in travel to any flybe. destination
Customer Service:	A minimum of two years experience in direct contact with the general public
Location:	Residential Requirements: Successful candidates must live within a maximum 60 minutes' travelling distance from their base airport.
How to apply	Visit website and apply on-line

GB Airways

Website:	www.gbairways.co.uk
Minimum Requirements:	
Education:	Educated to GCSE level with grade C in Maths and English (or equivalent)
Minimum Age:	Minimum age 19years
Height:	Minimum height 5'2" (158 cm)
Medical:	Medically fit to be cabin crew
Swimming:	Swim unaided a minimum of 25 meters and tread water
Passport:	Have the indefinite right to work in the UK and preferably have a valid EU passport
How to apply	Visit the website and download the application form – must complete in own handwriting.

Monarch

Website:	www.flymonarch.com
Minimum Requirements:	
Education:	A good standard of education (minimum of GCSE standard)
Minimum Age:	Minimum age 19
Height / Weight:	Height 160 - 187 cm with weight in proportion to height
Passport:	Holder of an EU passport (with unrestricted world-wide travel)
Medical:	A high standard of physical fitness
Swimming:	Capable of swimming 23 metres
Other:	The ability to converse with and have a genuine interest in people
How to apply	Visit website and download application form

My Travel

Website:	www.mytravel.com
Minimum Requirements:	
Education:	educated to GCSE level, including maths and English at grade C or above
Minimum Age:	aged 20 or over
Height / Weight::	between 5'2" and 6'3" in height with weight in proportion to height
Swimming:	Can swim 30 metres or more
Passport:	current UK/EU passport
How to apply	Request application form by e-mail from cabincrew.recruitment@mytravel.co.uk

Thomas Cook

Website:	www.thomascook.com
Minimum Requirements:	
Education:	Educated to at least GCSE standard or equivalent
Minimum Age:	Minimum age of 19 years
Languages:	Fluent in spoken and written English
Medical:	Physically fit to undertake flying duties A visual acuity of 6/9 with or without glasses
Height:	Height between 1.60m and 1.89 m (5ft 3" and up)
Customer Service:	Successful experience within a customer service environment
Passport:	An E.U. country passport and the unrestricted right to live and work in the UK and unrestricted entry into other countries
How to apply	visit website to complete an on-line application – or download application form

Virgin Atlantic

Website:	www.virgin-atlantic.com
Minimum Requirements:	
Education:	well educated
Minimum Age:	aged 19 years and over
Height / Weight:	stand at least 5'2" in height with weight in proportion
Passport:	hold an EU passport
Medical:	physically fit
How to apply	To receive an application form, call their recruitment desk 0870 190 4403

Note Pad

Note Pad

Note Pad

Note Pad